ACTUALIZATIONS:

YOU DON'T HAVE TO REHEARSE TO BE YOURSELF

12

ACTUALIZATIONS

YOU DON'T HAVE TO REHEARSE TO BE YOURSELF

By
STEWART EMERY
with
NEAL ROGIN

DOLPHIN BOOKS
Doubleday & Company, Inc.
Garden City, New York

A portion of this book, ACTUALIZATIONS: YOU DON'T HAVE TO REHEARSE TO BE YOURSELF, appeared in *New Age Journal* under the title "Union: Making Your Relationships Work," copyright © 1977 by Stewart Emery. "Our Relationship with Our Parents," "How to Transform Your Relationship with Your Children," and "Without Communication, There Is Nothing" have also appeared in *New Age Journal*, copyright © 1978 by Stewart Emery. In addition, "Transforming Our Romantic Relationships" has appeared in *New Woman* Magazine, copyright © 1978 by Stewart Emery.

Library of Congress Cataloging in Publication Data

Emery, Stewart, 1941–
  Actualizations.

  1. Self-actualization (Psychology) 2. Interpersonal relationships. I. Rogin, Neal, joint author. II. Title.
BF637.S4E46   158′.1

A Dolphin Books Original
Doubleday & Company, Inc.

ISBN: 0-385-13122-4
Library of Congress Catalog Card Number 77–76276
Copyright © 1977, 1978, by Stewart Emery
All rights reserved
Printed in the United States of America

To Carol, the spirit and energy source of Actualizations, who is to me a partner, and a friend.

ACKNOWLEDGMENTS

To my parents, for my presence on this earthly plane is a reflection of their love for one another.

To Jann, who discovered many paths that were timely for me to walk.

To Paul, who has allowed me to discover that children are wonderful, strong, responsible, and perceptively creative people.

To Werner, for a relationship that contributes so much to my education and experience.

To the Actualizations staff, for their support, and for being themselves.

To Neal, who turned our conversations into this book.

To the many, many people who, in opening themselves and their lives to me, are my teachers.

Thank you.

Stewart Emery, August 1977

CONTENTS

IV. OUR RELATIONSHIP WITH OUR PARENTS

V. THE TRANSFORMATION OF OUR RELA-
TIONSHIP WITH OUR BODY

VI. WITHOUT COMMUNICATION, THERE
IS NOTHING

VII. TRANSFORMING OUR ROMANTIC RELATIONSHIPS

XI. RELATIONSHIP WITH THE BOSS

XII. HOW TO TRANSFORM YOUR RELA-TIONSHIP WITH REALITY

XV

ACTUALIZATIONS:

YOU DON'T HAVE TO REHEARSE TO BE YOURSELF

I. PROLOGUE

The purpose of this book is to enable you to recognize the conditions that support the joyful workability of your relationships, and to contribute to your ability to create an environment in which your relationships become joyful, nurturing, satisfying adventures in mutual and personal growth.

Now, for most of us, exhilarating and satisfying adventures in growth seem like a fairy tale. Most of us would be happy if we could just get to the place where our relationships are not a source of pain and anguish.

To have our relationships become a source of joy and satisfaction, a reflection of our spiritual essence and of our love, would require nothing short of a complete transformation—and that is what this book is about.

It is about transforming our relationships. And not just our relationships with our husband or our wife, or with our boss or with our children. We are talking here about transforming our relationships with ourselves, our life, our work—about transforming our relationships with everything.

This may sound unrealistic. After all, how can we accomplish something that is as lofty as transformation by reading a book? Well, it is the idea that transformation is a rare and unusual occurrence that keeps it from becoming what it really is, our birthright.

In the Actualizations Workshop, Carol and I have had the privilege of being with thousands of people as they transform their relationships—in one weekend, in one day, in one instant. And they leave with an altered, fresh, workable, and alive way of relating to their lives. Their age, background, and belief do not matter. When people experience who they are as lovable and capable human beings, transformation is a natural result.

We wondered about that. We wondered why it is that when people discover that they are ultimately supportable, lovable, and capable, as they do in the workshop, everything changes. They transform; but transform from what? What is it that we think is true about us that we discover is not true? Is there one fundamental misconception we all have as human beings which keeps us from being individually and collectively successful as a species?

The Central Issue of Our Existence

Yes, it is the central issue of our existence. It is so fundamental to our experience as human beings that the only time we notice we have it is when, in some rare and magical moments, it suddenly disappears.

It is the experience of separation.

The experience of being human is the experience of being separate—of being unrelated, being outside of life, of needing to do something in order to make it. And the urge to assuage the feeling of separation has motivated civilization since time began.

The experience that we are separate is the source of our idea that we need an act in order to get by in the world. It is the root cause of our notion that who we are is simply not enough, that we have to lay something over the top of who we are in order to be all right.

"Well, then," we might say here, "if our problem is that we are separate, the solution seems obvious. End the separation. Find somebody and get into relationship. Find some way to heal the feeling of separation." A great idea. Except that we have been trying to accomplish this for thousands of years.

Our culture has more options, choices, and alternatives to quench the feeling of separation than any other in history. And yet, even with the Porsche or Mercedes in the garage of the summer home, even with all our achievements and acquisitions, at four o'clock in the morning the sense of separation still haunts our dreams.

We are coming to the important and difficult realization that more stuff, more relationships, more acquisitions will not extinguish the sense of separation. While it may seem to work for a little while, no form outside of ourselves is ever going to permanently heal that wound.

We cannot solve our problem of separation for the same reason we cannot blow out a picture of a candle.

Separation Is an Illusion

Separation is an illusion that we have made real by agreement. The fundamental nature of the universe is one of balance and harmony in relationship. There is *no* separation.

If there is no separation, where did we even get the idea? Let's just say here that that illusion is born when we are. Birth itself is an experience of separation; from that experience we build the illusion that we are separate, when in reality we are not.

We build our illusion out of a decision based upon a shortage of facts collected upon our entry into a reality that is new to us. We have no way of knowing that when we are born, our feeling of separation flows from an illusion that is built upon our lack of experience in the reality in which we find ourselves.

The physicalness of our predicament is very real. It is true that we can't make it alone in this world as babies. We cannot survive by ourselves. We feel alone and separate. But to come up with the conclusion that separation is fundamental to life based upon our limited observation is to tell ourselves a lie. We simply can't see that our feeling of being separate is a result of our limited perception of the true nature of the universe.

All our efforts to end our sense of separation are the attempt to solve a problem we do not have in the first place. Our life has become a collection of solutions to a problem we do not have.

Let us look at it another way. Being born is like waking up inside a dream and not knowing it. In our sleep we have amassed a garrison of devices and decisions to protect ourselves from the threat from outside. We seek to protect ourselves from all that we feel separate from. We have barricaded ourselves in our cabin to fight off the Indians while we wait in fervent hope for the cavalry to arrive and save us.

Well, I have good news and I have bad news. First, the bad news: the cavalry isn't coming. Sorry, but Rin Tin Tin, John Wayne, and the detachment from Fort Apache are not going to come riding over the hill. No one is going to save us from the Indians of our life.

When we really get the hopelessness of that fact, it may make us very sad. It will also allow us to get the good news. And the good news is, there aren't any Indians. There is only a universe that supports us in making life a joyful adventure or an endless nightmare. So while there is no hope, it is also true that there is no hope needed.

If that is true, then why does the world look the way it does? The answer is simple: we live in a universe that supports us, and we do not know that. We are under the dual illusion that there is somebody or something *out there* that is going to get us if we don't watch out (enter the Devil) and that there is somebody or something *out there* that is going to save us if we *do* watch out (enter God, Santa Claus, and an assorted cast of good guys). We see ourselves as ultimate victims—helpless pawns in a chess game between good and evil. None of this is happening, of course. We only think it is. And because we think it is happening, guess what? It is.

We all share the same misconception about who we are and about our separation, and out of that collective philosophical viewpoint we create a life on this planet that maintains the illusion of separation. Everything that flows out of a philosophy of separation makes it appear that there really is a separation.

Out of the illusion of separation and the need for protection we created weapons, and out of the weapons we created wars, which proved how right we were to have created weapons. So now there are millions dead, which proves conflict is a reality. It is real and it is tragic. And the reality of the millions of dead is so overpowering that nobody could own up to the fact that there are millions dead as a result of what was originally an illusion.

What we have is a planet of people who think they are

separate, banding together into larger forms of separateness called nations, in an endless and unsuccessful attempt to create an artificial sense of unity. Lost in the illusion that this will work, we are headed for disaster.

Freedom, as Krishnamurti pointed out, comes out of the experience that there are no alternatives. In other words, there is only one "the way things are." There is only one fundamental nature of the universe, in that we have no other alternatives. The only thing we have choice about is whether we are going to discover this or not. And after we have made this discovery we have the alternatives of whether we are going to live it or not. The continued existence of life on this planet will require that enough of us discover an enlightenment out of which can flow a social order in harmony with the fundamental nature of the universe.

What we have in the world today are not relationships but conflicts. And all conflict between people is a conflict of personal reality. We do not all perceive the world in the same way. And we regard the fact that somebody sees an aspect of reality different from the way we see it, as a threat. We don't seem to realize that whatever reality each of us has is a part of everything and is not all of everything.

Your reality is a valid, essential, and magnificent aspect of the whole, and so is mine. At the same time, your reality is not all of the whole, and neither is mine. If we can recognize that our own reality—the way we perceive life—is a part of everything, we can experience that we are not separate. You cannot be separate when you are a part of everything. If we can also see that our reality does not embrace all of everything, then we have the opportunity to grow to greater and greater wisdom.

Imagine for a moment that you and I are standing at opposite ends of a room. In the middle of the room, suspended in the air between us, is a large bicolored ball which represents "everything." But we don't know that it is bicolored. The part of the ball you can see is red, so you would say, "Stewart, that ball is red." On my side, I see only blue, so I would say "Wrong! The ball is blue." And the argument we have come to call human interaction would ensue. I proclaim my view of everything to be all of everything, and you proclaim your view of everything to be all of everything. We fail to recognize that the way you see the world and the way I see the world adds dimension to each other's vision.

The Actualizations Workshop is an environment that supports people in breaking through the illusion of separation to the reality of our relatedness. Something happens over the course of those four days that cannot be explained or adequately described. People experience the dissolution of the illusion of separateness and the revelation of our fundamental and undeniable unity. The illusion of separation gives way to the opening of the heart and unconditional love.

When we clear away the clouds of separation, we can see that all the solutions for our problems in life, all the reasons we have to explain why we are the way we are, all the stories and scenarios we have constructed to justify our lives and to excuse our shortcomings—all those things disappear. They become unnecessary and pointless, like a candle after the sun comes up.

In light of the experience of the reality of our relationship with everything, the illusion of our separation is revealed and disappears. And in that timeless moment, we see that we are as we are and we are ultimately enough. We are *magnificent*, and we have been preoccupied with trying to be *okay*.

How we got that way, how we can wake up from the dream, and what to do after we wake up, are what this book is about.

II. WHO ARE WE, ANYWAY?

Some Basic Psychology

This book is not intended to become a textbook on psychology. It's a handbook to read and use that will allow you to transform the quality of your relationships. Your relationships can be joyful, satisfying, and fulfilling adventures. Relationships that are joyful and nurturing must be built on foundations that are workable. The most fundamental foundation is our model of what it is to be a person.

Throughout history there have been a few social transformations. They have all depended upon an altered model of what it means to be a person. The society evolves to support the emergent model of man.

So let us examine some models. We are not going to attempt to establish which model is right. We will simply observe the model and consider whether or not it is a suitable foundation upon which to build our relationships.

You and I: the Religious Model

Somewhere along the way the religions that have most influenced our existence developed the notion of original sin.

If we look at the history of human experience we will see that, for the most part, civilization has been an endless desert of suffering, sparsely dotted with an occasional oasis of relative peace, freedom, and happiness.

The reality is that most of the people who have lived have had to struggle with disease, famine, oppression, deprivation, and endless fear, punctuated with periods of terror. In short, the quality of life has not been filled with love, kindness, joy, and happiness.

It is a human addiction to require an explanation for the way things are. With regard to the quality of human life, original sin is an enormously convenient explanation for the fact that life does not work. The rationale goes something like this: Your life is full of suffering as a consequence of your heritage of evil thoughts and deeds. It is suggested that in previous incarnations you and your people did terrible things and you are now suffering the consequences. If you suffer with grace, patience, and dignity, you will live happily ever after you die.

BULLSHIT!

Have you ever considered that if you get to the end of an unhappy, unsatisfying life as a member of the living dead and you discover that this was all there is, that you would be very angry?

The model of you and me as original sinners leaves us with the belief that suffering is our natural state. It is the nature of beliefs to be self-fulfilling prophecies. If you believe that you have done terrible things in the past and must suffer in consequence, then suffer you will. It makes no difference whether you are conscious of holding this belief or not; if you have the belief it will be fulfilled. If enough people in a society hold the belief, then the belief becomes the conscious or unconscious social reality, and the society will suffer.

If our life and relationships are going to work, we will have to accept that while we may not be certain of the purpose of our existence, we are not in this life to suffer. Be clear that I am not saying that there will be no suffering, or that suffering is either damaging or beneficial. I am saying that suffering is not the purpose of our existence.

Just because we were born in suffering does not mean we were born to suffer.

You and I: the Freudian Model

We developed the science called physics to provide us with certainty in our relationships with physical reality.

We developed the sciences of biology and medicine to provide us with certainty in the fields of organic existence and the health of the human body.

It is a human addiction to acquire certainty, so at the past turn of the century a science called psychology had began to emerge. The purpose of psychology was to provide us with an understanding of what it is to be a person, an understanding that leads us to joyful, satisfying lives.

The theories and teachings of Sigmund Freud represent the first force in psychology. While no doubt Freud would be horrified to be considered under the heading of spiritual leaders, there is much about him that places him in the category.

To understand Freud and his teachings, we should examine the climate and environment in which they emerged. Freud's theories developed in a climate of stifling Victorian prudery and a Europe dominated by the Church. They were revolutionary times—Europe was headed toward the First World War. Freudianism and psychoanalysis tore away at the blanket of Victorian prudery and represented a new model of what it meant to be a person: it was a radical philosophical outlook.

Freud taught that while we prided ourselves on the quality of reason, thus separating ourselves from the animals, the quality of reason was purely illusionary.

Freud stated that we only seemed to act in reasonable terms, while in fact we acted out of old, hidden, irrational, and unconscious motives. He took the point of view that by nature you and I are motivated by powerful sexual, animalistic, and destructive urges. This basic nature Freud called the *id*. The process of growing up to become usefully part of society required that we develop mechanisms to suppress our incestuous, homicidal, and cannibalistic wishes. The control allows us the veneer of socially acceptable behavior Freud labeled the *superego*. The process of our life was one of conflict between the id and the superego, the classic battle between good and evil: the "good" of the acquired veneer of socially acceptable behavior and the "evil" of our incestuous, cannibalistic, and environmentally destructive nature. The battle rages, according to Freud, in a part of the mind he labeled the *ego*. The result of the battle was manifested in the form of our behavior. If our behavior is acceptable, the superego is winning; if unacceptable, then the id is winning.

What we have is a model not too different from the

religious model we've just explored. We have the notion that we are incestuous, cannibalistic, and destructive, which sounds pretty much like the equivalent of sin. Also, we have the concept of the torment of the struggle between the id and the superego, which parallels the notion that living is about suffering. Not a very promising model for building a science to elevate the quality of the experience of living.

You and I: the Behaviorist Model

The second force in psychology is known as behavior modification, or behaviorism. The behaviorist theory is ascribed to two men, B. F. Skinner and John Watson. They did not argue philosophically with Freud's theory. Perhaps they thought what we ought to do is get human behavior cleaned up. We'd better come up with a way of modifying behavior. All we have to do is put together a way of creating super superegos and we will all live happily ever after.

Obviously, the solution was to come up with defense mechanisms and suppression mechanisms that absolutely work all the time to keep the revelation of the animalism, cannibalism, and all that other nasty stuff beneath the surface. They figured that if we can do that, everything will work out. Thus, the behavior modification engineers set out to find ways to modify human behavior. And they did it. Behavior modification works. But as someone has pointed out, so does torture.

The really hard-core behaviorists believe that the practice of behavior modification on a grand scale is the only answer to the continuation of human existence on this planet. It is important to know that there are behaviorists today who think that all of us should be subjected to behavior modification, and they are working on computer models that would make this possible. Their argument is this: We are all in fact a product of behavior modification. Your life and my life are absolutely the reflection of the influences of the process of conditioning. The problem is, they say, that the processes of modification and conditioning that we have been exposed to have been random and unworkable. So since we are the product of behavior modification anyway, wouldn't it make sense to take the randomness out of it and just do it right? Wouldn't it make sense to make sure we are not exposed to conditioning that does not work and come up with a unified model that does work?

Well, intellectually that may sound attractive. But if we look, we would probably prefer the randomness of our conditioning to conditioning that was scientifically administered by a computer bank.

What the behaviorists are telling us is this: Give us your children at birth, and in sixteen years we'll give you back a person with behavior and personality custom-made to your order. In sixteen years we can give you an Albert Schweitzer, and Attila the Hun, an Albert Einstein, an Adolf Hitler, a Mary Baker Eddy, or a Cleopatra. Just fill out the multiple-choice order form, drop off your child, and come back to the will-call counter in sixteen years. This is the implicit statement of the hard-line behaviorists. But let's set that aside for a moment and consider the theory itself, since whether we like it or not, you and I are a product of the process of conditioning that started at our birth and has continued through our lifetime.

The first postulate of behavior modification is this: If somebody does something for which he or she receives positive acknowledgment, or positive reinforcement, he is more likely to repeat the behavior. Any behavior that is positively acknowledged is likely to be repeated.

The next piece of information is more interesting, however. It says, if you do something and nobody takes any notice of it at all, you are less likely to do it again. In other words, any behavior that is consistently ignored will ultimately cease. (You have to recognize that these are all tendencies, not absolutes.)

The most fascinating piece of information has to do with negative acknowledgment, or punishment. If you do something and you are punished—negatively acknowledged—the results of the negative acknowledgment are unpredictable, *except* under circumstances wherein the only kind of acknowledgment you ever get is negative; then negative acknowledgment will lead to a repetition of the behavior that was negatively acknowledged. If, when you were growing up, the only time you got acknowledged was when you did something that your parents did not like, then the administration of negative acknowledgment, or punishment, led you to continue to repeat behavior that led to your getting punished. Under conditions in which negative acknowledgment is the only kind of acknowledgment you get, negative acknowledgment will lead to an increase in behavior that will reproduce negative acknowledgment. That is probably the most important piece of information that anybody who raises children, manages people, or teaches can get. Let's look at the consequences.

It is most obvious in our penal system. People are in jail because they did something that got negatively acknowledged. The reasons they do things that get negatively acknowledged is that they think that is the only way they can ever get any kind of attention. The more we give them negative acknowledgment, the more negative behavior they will manifest. It is a situation in which there is no way to win.

Look in our own lives. One of the things that becomes very clear to people in the workshop is that society is an en-

vironment that supports endarkenment, not enlighten...
The social reality of people's lives supports their journey
into darkness, not their evolution toward an enlightened and
joyful view of the world. As babies, we learn that the most
reliable way to get acknowledgment is to make a fuss. If we
wave our arms and legs and scream at the top of our lungs,
somebody will take notice of us. That teaches us one of life's
most important lessons: If we are a pain in the ass, we will
get noticed. The other important lesson we learn as a child
is that if we get sick, we will be treated as a person. In our
society, when we talk about raising children, we are really
talking about driving them crazy. What education is about
is conditioning people to be irresponsible and stupid. It
teaches them to be skillful technologists and useless people,
because we have a system of conditioning that says the way
to get acknowledged is to get sick or become an absolute
pain in the ass.

In our society, if you manifest behavior that happens to be
workable, the probability is that nobody will notice. There
is no consistent reward for workable behavior; it seems as
though there is no reward for behaving in an enlightened
way. We are all a product of random, insane conditioning.

You and I: the Humanistic Model

So far, all the models of you and me are models that could
not possibly support an image of ourselves as lovable and
capable beings.

Humanistic psychology grew in part out of a revolution
against the psychoanalytical model of people as being nothing more than a sick outcome of the battle between our
animalistic essence and a repressive social veneer, and in

part against the behavioral therapists' detached, dehumanizing model of man.

Humanistic psychology is referred to as the third force in psychology, and the concept of the third force is often expanded to include what has come to be called the "human potential movement."

Three of the most charismatic forces of the movement have been Abraham Maslow, Carl Rogers, and Fritz Perls—the visionary, the saint, and the superstar of humanistic psychology. We will focus on Maslow's contribution.

Abraham Maslow was one of the first to recognize that everything we knew about people was based upon the study of the mentally ill and the criminally insane together with the observation of the behavior of mice, dogs, pigeons, and a handful of college students. Hardly an appropriate foundation for a science that promised a transformation in the quality of human experience! Distortion and unworkability must follow from looking to evil as a model of our future, or to the behavior of animals as a source of understanding the nature of our behavior.

Maslow had the vision to observe that psychology had become too much concerned with sorrow and sickness and not with joy and health, too concerned with the process of degeneration and destruction rather than transformation and growth. He reasoned that all we are likely to learn from studying what doesn't work about life is how to be an expert at what doesn't work in life. Maslow noted that is pretty much a description of the human condition.

He chose therefore to study the creatively intelligent aspects of people that supported life's being a joyful adventure. Maslow concerned himself with the person as a unique and individual being whose qualities of humanness must not be lost in the process of a science that viewed us as evil and sought to reduce our behavior to some mechanically predictable system that washes the passion out of life. If what we want to do is become creatively talented at making our life a joyful, satisfying tribute to what works, we should study the lives of people whose lives work.

Abraham Maslow's great contribution to psychology and to life itself is his model of the self-actualizing person. The word actualize means to make real through action. Thus, self-actualizing people are those who are continually discovering avenues of action that provide them with an unfolding, real, joyful experience of their own creative humanness. Their action, focused in the light of human consciousness, becomes of service to themselves, other people, and the world. As you read the qualities of those whom Maslow described as being self-actualized, in a very real practical way you will discover they sound like qualities you would like to experience within yourself.

The Qualities of Self-actualized People

Self-actualized people have the quality of being real. In other words they do not spend their time pretending to be something they are not. Their life is just the way it appears to be, the way in which they conduct themselves is open and whole and they have a passion for living. These people have an enormous ability to get along with other people and are not threatened by other people who hold a different view of the world than themselves. They see opportunities in situations and events rather than seeing threatening problems, and they are not concerned with what others think of them.

People committed to self-actualization take a broad view of life and the world and at the same time are very moved by simple pleasures. They see the uniqueness in each moment, the sunset of this moment being unique and complete, not to be compared with other sunsets; this rose a unique and individual rose, to be enjoyed without automatic comparison to other roses.

Self-actualizing people are capable of profound and movingly beautiful relationships. They are not *afraid of commitment* and have a degree of mastery of themselves and life that makes their commitment to people or to a project truly worth something. They have the ability to allow you to like yourself more by simply being in their presence.

Most people, when faced with some decision about expressing their feelings or taking up some challenge, find it too easy to back off, telling themselves that this is neither the time nor the place and that it would be better to wait. People on the path to self-actualization resolve similar situations by making a growth choice rather than the fear choice. They are willing to take risks.

Maslow's point of view was that it is our inherent nature to pursue self-actualization. He took the viewpoint that we are by nature loving, open, creative, intelligent beings with a passionate desire for growth and to joyfully make a contribution to ourselves, other people, and the world.

Self-actualization is not an image of a psychological elite. The implicit statement is that each of us can take charge of his own life in a way that will lead him to experience a deeper sense of joy, satisfaction, and fulfillment. The promise is that ecstasy is available to everyone.

According to Maslow's estimates, only about 2 per cent of individuals in this society achieve self-actualization. Now we have a fundamentally important question to ask: If it is true that by nature we are open, loving, passionate, and creatively intelligent beings committed to self-actualization, why is it that only 2 per cent of us make it to the state of self-actualization? Why is it that 98 per cent of us end up conforming more to the Freudian model than to the model of the self-actualized being?

Maslow's answer is "environmental factors." The answer is both true and useless. Let us now go on to explore another model that we have developed in conducting the Actualizations Workshop. It is simply called the Actualizations model. (Notice that the word "self" does not appear.)

You and I: the Actualizations Model

In conducting the Actualizations Workshop, our concern is never with esoteric truth. We are simply concerned with moving a person's life toward a more joyful and satisfying experience of himself, other people, and the world. Thus, in a very pragmatic way, what becomes important is a model of what it is to be a person which serves the individual's growth as a joyful, conscious being.

It may very well be true that neither Freud's nor Maslow's model of what it means to be a person is in fact valid. At the practical level of working with people, however, one thing becomes very clear: It is not possible to support a person growing toward a joyful and satisfying and productive experience of himself in life if one starts with the assumption that the individual is incestuous, animalistic, environmentally destructive, and generally evil. If the quality of a person's life is to be enriched, we have to view him as a joyful, open, communicative, lovable, and capable person who has not yet fully realized that about himself.

The value in Maslow's model is that it supports the growth of the individual and the workability of society.

Moreover, the model's usefulness is not dependent on the fact that we are inherently, by nature, that way. There is a fair amount of evidence to support that we are not inherently either good or evil. We are simply born with an enormous amount of potential. At birth this potential is not actualized; in other words, none of the potential has as yet been made real through action. It appears that the purpose of this potential is to equip us to respond creatively to the environment in order to secure our existence as a species on the planet. We will use our creative potential or creative intelligence to develop qualities that serve us in the environment in which we exist. In this sense, Maslow's answer to why so few of us ever attain self-actualization is accurate. If the environmental conditions surrounding our life support our evolution toward self-actualization, we will move in that direction. If the environmental conditions in our life don't support this movement, then we won't. Let's state this principle in another way.

If you were a willow tree living by a riverside, the environmental conditions of your existence would support your evolution toward becoming a self-actualized willow tree. We wouldn't have to do anything to insure your growth as a willow tree in this environment. In other words, your relationship with the environment would result in you developing all the qualities one would expect to see in a self-actualized willow tree. Of course, the process is not entirely riskless. Somebody may cut you down to build a freeway. However, the chances that you would make it all the way to self-actualization would be extraordinarily high. If, on the other hand, you were a willow tree and you were planted in the desert, the chances of your making it as a self-actualized willow tree would be virtually nil. The environmental conditions of your existence simply wouldn't allow it. It wouldn't make any difference if you really wanted to be a self-actualized willow tree. The environmental conditions simply wouldn't support it, and it wouldn't happen.

It is very important to see the simplicity of this example before we go on. On a very fundamental level, what is true for the willow tree is true for you and me. If we are in an environment that supports our evolution toward self-actualization, then it will happen, and if we are not, then it won't happen. However, you and I have some qualities that the willow tree does not possess.

The willow tree does not possess qualities or attributes that allow it to select its environment. In other words, a willow tree that finds itself planted in the desert cannot hail a passing yellow cab and ask the driver to take it to the riverside. You and I, on the other hand, can. So now we come to an important principle.

You and I have within us the creative intelligence to recognize the conditions of existence that support our growth toward self-actualization, and we have the wherewithal to place ourselves in such an environment. If the environmental conditions that support our growth are not immediately available, then we have the creative ability to bring these conditions into existence and then live in them. Thus we have a very unique relationship with reality. The quality of our experience of living is a reflection of the environmental conditions of our life, and as human beings we have the potential and creative ability to recognize and construct environmental conditions that support our well-being. If we fail to recognize this principle and apply it, and persist in seeing ourselves as victims of an environment over which we have no control, then we will lead a colorless existence as members of the living dead. In other words, we *can* have relationships that work. It is possible. Let us further examine the quality of creative intelligence.

Creative Intelligence

We live in a society in which we have accepted that education is a solution to a higher quality of life. It is. The trouble is, however, that we have never discovered what the word education means. The word comes from the Latin *educare,* which means "to draw out of." Thus education should draw people out of themselves. It should provide people with an opportunity to grow in the areas of self-esteem and capability, in compassion for life and a compassion for living.

Since we never discovered what the meaning of the word education is, we invented a meaning. We invented the meaning "drum into" in place of the meaning "draw out of." As Peter Drucker points out, "When a subject becomes totally obsolete, we make it a required course." At the end of the "educational" process we have become technically semicompetent human machines, and as creative human beings we have turned into morons.

Being semicompetent human machines allows us to turn on the morning coffee, drive on the freeway with semisafety, and go to the supermarket. We can become some sort of professional machine and get a job that just about allows us to pay for the coffee percolator, the automobile, and the groceries.

We may even become brilliantly competent human machines, and thus be able to alter the physical environment and land a man on the moon and a television camera on Mars. Unfortunately, this kind of education leaves us incompetent in the area of human relationships. It leaves us hopelessly unprepared to be together in a loving, compassionate, joyful, and constructive way.

We require a special kind of intelligence if we are going to be able to relate to one another successfully. We have to reacquire the ability to see each event or situation as unique and individual. Then we have to be able to respond to the event or situation in a unique and appropriate way. Sadly we rarely do this. Instead we relate to a person today the way we remember him being the last time we saw him. If he is the same in this moment as he was in the past, okay. If he is not, then the way we attempt to relate in this moment will be inappropriate. If we are meeting someone for the first time, what we do is relate to him based upon some model of whom or what he represents to us, or whom he reminds us of. If the model we have is accurate, okay. If it is not, then the way in which we will attempt to relate will be inappropriate.

If we are going to relate in a way that works, we have to be able to view this moment together as a unique and individual moment, and respond to this moment creatively, in a unique and individual way. The degree to which we are able to do this is the measure of our creative human intelligence.

Let's Kill Some Sacred Cows in the Arena of Human Growth

As human beings, we are addicted to certainty; we are also addicted to comfort. We now come upon another addiction: We are addicted to beliefs. This addiction is very evident in the field of human growth. I will review some of the most popular ideas.

One belief that keeps cropping up is that a desire to grow is an admission that we are not all right to begin with. I remember a time that if you admitted you were going to see a psychiatrist, everybody thought you were crazy. We have seen an almost complete reversal of this belief in some areas of the country; if you are not going to a psychiatrist, people conclude that you *must* be crazy. In spite of this reversal, we frequently encounter the person that says, "If I express an interest in my own growth, which will first require an examination of my life, then I will be required to admit that there is something wrong with me and that I am not all right the way I am." Absolutely not so. *The nature of growth is that we go forward from where we are. This in no way requires that we make a value judgment regarding where we are. We need only recognize that there is more available to us in life and then make a commitment to reach for it.*

Another all-time favorite belief is that the exploration of the past will automatically lead to an enrichment of the future. Sometimes this is expressed as the belief that it is absolutely necessary to explore the past in order to grow as we move along into the future. Nonsense!

I personally know people who have spent thousands and thousands of dollars in the exploration of their past, believing that in so doing they would transform the quality of their present life and insure for themselves a future that exceeded their fondest dreams. All too often they end up with nothing more than a cast-iron alibi for being the way they are. The reasons and beliefs they have collected act as a barrier to their growth rather than insuring it.

The power to grow exists in this moment, not in the past. If we go back to the analogy of the willow tree, we discover that all we need to grow is an environment that supports our growth.

It is sometimes true that an exploration of our past allows us to recognize those periods of our lives in which we have lived in an environment that has supported our growth and also to recognize those periods in our lives when this has not been true. Thus, as a result of such exploration, we have available to us from the wealth of our own experience a working model of what supports us and what doesn't. The model is useful only if we use the exploration of our past to go forward, surrounding ourselves with a climate that works for us.

Be clear that it is in no way necessary to explore the past to discover what would work for us now. Sometimes it is useful, and just as often it isn't.

Another popularly held notion is that an understanding of why we are the way we are will automatically produce growth. This is similar to the belief surrounding the exploration of the past. In order to grow in a healthy, joyful, and productive way, we must first accept the way we are. We must be able to notice ourselves and the way we are and view this compassionately. If we do come to an understanding of why we are the way we are, and we use it to develop compassion for ourselves and for other people, then the understanding we have come to is of service. Such compassion avoids wasting energy and consciousness in putting ourselves down. It allows us to give up dwelling on our errors and mistakes, thus freeing our creative intelligence and energy for action.

Understanding alone, however, does not produce any results. We can explore the past forever and come up with the most wonderful theories about how we got to be where we are. But none of it is useful unless we use the information as a foundation upon which to build, *by action*, the conditions that support our growth and well-being.

Another all-time favorite belief is that growth has to be

inful. I have met so many people in the human potential movement who believe that if what they are doing is not painful, then they are not getting any value. Again I say, Nonsense! Of course, if you are addicted to pain and suffering and the thought of growth being a joyful adventure is unacceptable to you, then by all means continue to suffer. After all, that is your privilege.

We need to explore at this point our relationship with comfort and discomfort. Although I don't care for the translation of experiments with animals to human implications, the following example is useful. A lot of research has been done in exploration of the conditions that support the growth of amoebas. Now, amoebas have never been very popular as pets, but an observation of their nature and response to changing conditions in their environment has made available some information of enormous importance and relevance to human life. Researchers have discovered that if you place an amoeba in an environment in which it is subjected to a great deal of discomfort, it will die. This is perhaps not at all surprising; the same is true of you and me. If you and I dwell in an environment that subjects us to constant discomfort, to pain, to constant put-downs and belittlement, our spirit for living will die. The surprise comes when we examine the results of placing an amoeba in an environment that provides it with absolute and continuous comfort. The result is the death of the amoeba. Again, there is a direct parallel with the results of a similar situation in human life. If you and I give in to an addiction for comfort, our spirit for life will die. If our spirit for living dies, we will find ways to arrange that our bodies also die.

Researchers discovered that if an amoeba was to evolve and become a self-actualized amoeba, it needed to exist in an environment made up of a careful balance of comfort and discomfort; the same is absolutely true for you and me.

If we are to reach the state of self-actualization, it will be along a path paved with a balance of comfort and discomfort.

At first reading, this may not seem very attractive. Nobody other than a confirmed masochist is in a hurry to pursue activities that are uncomfortable. What I observe as true for those people who are committed to a path of growth is that their experience of discomfort is exhilarating in a very healthy way. These people are excited about making the growth choice rather than constantly seeking the protection of the fear choice. These people find as they travel down the path that discomfort is sometimes a companion, though seldom for extensive periods. And on the other side of discomfort they discover a new high waiting for them, together with a deeper sense of their own self-worth.

III. HOW WE GOT TO BE THE WAY WE ARE, AND THE TRANSFORMATION OF OUR RELATIONSHIP WITH OURSELVES

OF OUR RELATIONSHIP
WITH OURSELVES

Everything you wanted to know about yourself but were afraid to ask.

The Birth of Separation

If you are looking for the source of our problems, you might say that our first mistake was getting born. But to see why our birth has turned out to be such a problem for us, let's start a little before birth.

Life Before Birth

Before we got born, we were living in a super little apartment. We didn't have to worry about anything; everything was taken care of for us. It was warm, it was comfortable, the climate was perfectly even; the room service was terrific; all the food and everything else we needed were piped in; there were no loud noises and very few intrusions.

Then, for a reason we don't understand, we get evicted. And the eviction is, to say the least, an unpleasant shock. We start off by being forced down a passageway that is inherently too small. Our head pops out into a world that's noisy, brightly lit, and 26 degrees colder than where we've just come from. Somebody grabs hold of us (our first experience of contact) and pulls. We get held up in the air by our ankles, so our first experience of gravity is upside down. Then somebody cuts off our life-support system, slaps our back, and for the first time, we have to gasp for air. We are also aware that our mother, the landlady, is having a very difficult time for herself.

After we are separated from our little apartment, we get put into a much bigger place, now filled with other little bodies the same size as ours, all making a lot of noise.

Now we find we have to struggle and work to get anything to eat, elimination is messy, and breathing itself is hard work. We become immediately aware that we are not in a world that appears to be custom-made for our convenience.

So the very first experience we have in life is one of separation. The birth experience itself is an experience of separation. So life, to us, equals separation.

In the womb there was no separation. We were absolutely one with the environment. Suddenly, we experience that we are separate and that we can't make it by ourselves. We experience that there are others, separate from us, and that our well-being depends upon them. If they don't like us, we are in deep trouble.

Our perception tells us that our well-being is dependent on an external source, in this case our mother and we decide to accept this. Here lies the beginning of our error—the birth of the illusion of separation.

So now we are here, and we've got to make it in the world. Somebody has to feed us, care for us, change our diapers, turn us over—somebody has to do everything for us. So we immediately begin to look around for somebody who can make it turn out for us.

Now, that would seem to us to be our mother's duty. But, remember, she's just evicted us. So at best our relationship with our mother is off to a shaky start.

It may be good to stop here for a moment and notice that we grow up with a very distorted idea about our rights and privileges in life, and about the way things are supposed to be. However, the way things are is not the real problem. It is how we feel about the way things are. Let's put it this way: The quality of our life is a function of how we feel about the way things are; or how we feel about what we think happened to us. And we usually do not feel good about our birth. Getting born was okay; it's how we feel about getting born. It is the crazy decisions we make about the events of our life that determine what our life will be like.

A Ticket to the Show

Getting born is like being given a ticket to the theatrical event called life. It's like going to the theater. Now, all that ticket will get you, is through the door. It doesn't get you a good time and it doesn't get you a bad time. You go in and sit down and you either love the show or you don't. If you do, terrific. And if you don't—that's show business.

Getting born into life is like that. But we don't understand it. We seem to be conditioned from a very early age that life should carry a Sears, Roebuck warranty, and that if we don't like some part of it we should be able to get that part of our life cheerfully refunded. We think that getting born should automatically guarantee us a great time. And we think that if we complain loudly enough, the nice lady behind the cashier's counter will cheerfully refund that period of our life so we can get something that will make us happier. Sorry, it does not work that way.

What Do We Do When Life Is No Fun?

All we are able to be at birth is ourselves. Nothing else is actualized. Only we are actualized; we can be ourselves. It's not so much that we know how to be ourselves; it's just that we don't know how to be *other* than ourselves. All we know how to be is just the way we are. We haven't developed the façades, the pretenses, the act, yet. So by definition we are ourselves, because we don't know any better—or should I say, we don't know any worse.

Other than that, we don't know anything. We don't know how to survive; we don't know how to live; we don't know how to relate; we don't know how to communicate; we don't know how to be a nuclear physicist, or a biologist, or an anthropologist; *we don't know how to do anything*.

We are born just with this enormous potential for experience. We have an enormous creative potential, with which to respond to our experience, to enhance the quality of our existence. And that is it.

On the level of physical reality, it's apparent to us that our well-being is in fact dependent on others. At birth this is inescapable. Naturally, what starts to be assembled in our own mind is a reality that says that how well off we are in the world is a function of other people's taking care of us. We start to get conditioned that if we were left to our own devices, we wouldn't make it. And not making it is not a whole lot of fun. So we call that level of experience "no fun." And what it feels like is a generalized pervasive anxiety over whether life is going to turn out. Once this feeling has been around for a while, we no longer notice that it is there, and yet now it is always there.

The Form Junkie

It is true that, as babies, if we were left alone it would definitely not turn out. As babies, we are very clear that we are dependent on others.

So the first thing we do is to look around for whatever we need for life to turn out for us. Of course, that is, Mother. Mother is supposed to make life turn out for us. But can she be trusted? She just evicted us, you remember. Not only that, as we get a little smarter we begin to look at Mother and wonder if she can make life turn out for herself.

We are conditioned from the very beginning that either Mother or Father or somebody other than us is going to insure that our life is wonderful, happy, and beautiful. As we grow up, we are given all sorts of stories and fantasies about the external sources that are going to save our ass and in some way assure us a happy ever-after.

There were the Tooth Fairy, the Easter Bunny, Superman, Tinkerbell, and the Lone Ranger. But most of all, there was Santa Claus. No matter how terrible it had been the rest of the year, somehow, on the twenty-fifth of December, Santa Claus was going to make it all better again. And it worked—until the toys broke, a week or two later.

After a time, we are told that there is no Santa Claus, *really*. But that does not stop us from believing that some source outside of us is going to make it all turn out. We still believe in Santa Claus at some level. Even as an adult, it looks to us as though our well-being is dependent on someone else.

We are all "form junkies." A form is anything that is not essence or experience or abstraction. Forms are activities or acquisitions. Forms are such things as beliefs, ceilings, automobiles, work, jogging, playing tennis, relationships—all those things are forms. For example, people are crazy when it comes to the form of a relationship—what it looks like to them. They measure it by strange standards of activities and acquisitions. "Well, if it's a good relationship, we should be screwing so many times a week, and she should cook me dinner, and I should be making this much money, and I should feel this certain way, and we should have a big house and two automobiles and a great stereo, etc."

The mental equation of form junkism goes something like this: "Life is no fun, but there is something outside of me—a form—that will make it all right. There is Hope." A form junkie is a prisoner of Hope.

Hope is the expectation that some source external to ourselves is going to save our ass so we will live happily over after. Hope is the confirmed belief in Santa Claus on some level. Hope is what keeps all the suffering in place.

Hopelessness is finding out that it is up to you. But nobody wants to know that. That would mean giving up whatever form of Santa Claus we have become attached to—whether it is the beautiful Fairy Princess we are going to marry, or the Handsome Prince who is going to sweep us off our feet, or the Fairy Godmother who is going to make it all better.

In America, we are convinced that if our marriage stinks, and our life in bed is a disaster, then all we have to do is put a Coke machine in the bedroom and things will go better. And the reality is that things do not go better with Coke; in fact, nutritionally, they go worse.

And men who doubt their masculinity are sold on the notion that if they smoke Marlboros, they can ride a horse and get laid at the same time. When in fact you won't ride a horse and get laid; you may end up with lung cancer and emphysema, which falls a long way short of the image in the dream. So we go from one form of Santa Claus to another, always believing that something external will be the answer to our prayers.

Our lives seem to be a series of pursuits of the things we were told would make life go better. Things will go better with Mother. Things will go better with an education. Things will go better with a wife. Things will go better with a husband. Things will go better with kids. Things will go better with a divorce. Things will go better with a pay increase. Things will go better with my own business. Things will go better with a Ph.D. Everyone is running around looking for the right form with which things will go better. We see our well-being as completely and absolutely dependent on form—on something external.

All this leads to disillusionment and mistrust, because, ultimately, no form of activity or acquisition can deliver what we think it will deliver. So we go from one disappointment to another, getting more and more disillusioned with it all and finding new ways to suppress our disillusionment, but all the while keeping alive the glimmer of hope. There is something that will do it.

One would think that, after all this disappointment, we would see through the game and just stop playing. But we don't, for a very good reason. There is something that keeps the game alive. I call it "temporary well-being."

Temporary Well-being—the Carrot We Run After

Our individual personal reality—the way we think life is and the part we are to play in it—is self-created. We put together our own personal reality. It is made up of our interpretation of our perceptions of the way things are and what has happened to us. We make some basic decisions about life when we are being born, and we add to the script and embellish it during our childhood. We end up with a view of ourselves and the world that is usually highly inaccurate, because our perceptions at an early age are not accurate. And, of course, the decisions we make about our perceptions are certainly not accurate. Out of that we put together our personal view of the world, and then we put together an environment that is a perfect reflection of our view of the world.

We write our script by the time we are about seven years old. Then we treat the world as if it were the back lot at Universal Studios. We pick out our sets and our props. We call Central Casting and send for extras. We go to Wardrobe, which may be Sears or Macy's or Saks Fifth Avenue, and choose our costumes. We select a location and begin filming the story of life as we see it, starring US. We literally create a reality that reflects our view of the world and who we are in relation to it.

If we have a reality that says that life is about suffering and struggle, we will create a life experience that proves our reality is accurate. If we have a personal reality that says our well-being is dependent on others, we will arrange for life to support our reality of dependency.

Thus, on some level we are out in the world creating a reality that accurately reflects our notion of the way life is. Out of the infinite number of possible experiences, emotions, and events that are available, we will pick just the ones that reflect our world view.

Now, most of us are not aware of our personal reality. It is held in our consciousness beneath our level of perception. For example, we may think that life is terrible, but we never notice that we think that life is terrible. We just go around creating experiences that back up our notion that life is terrible.

It is easy to see why someone might put together a personal reality that says that life is terrible, because for many of us, birth was terrible. So the decision that life is terrible becomes the context for our life. It is the bowl in which our life gets held. Everything that happens—the content of our life—gets held in a bowl that says life is terrible.

Now, what do you suppose someone to whom life was terrible would do about that? He will seek some form, something or someone outside of himself, to relieve the terribleness. We begin to look around for something that things will go better with. And, of course, we find something. And, lo and behold, things *do* go better! Amazing! Things actually seem to go better. At least the content of our life seems to improve. Say we find a new relationship. "This one is IT! I can feel it! I am so in love!" and everything is great—for a while. But the elation does not last. And once again something that started out bright and shiny and promising and hopeful ends up in an arguing, miserable, heart-rending breakup, or at best, a disappointment and disillusionment.

"What happened? Where did I go wrong?" we ask. Well, the answer is simple, but not easy. Our notion that life is terrible—the context our life is held in—is a much bigger and more powerful creative (in a negative way) force than the idea that things will go better with a new relationship. It's like trying to start a fire in a wet prairie. The little positive energy flow gets devoured by our more primary consideration, that life is terrible. If it begins to actually get good, that threatens our original notion that life is terrible, so we find (unconsciously) some devious way to muck it up.

It is that little rush of hope, that feeling of "maybe this time," that keeps us going from one disappointment to another. I call it temporary well-being. It feels good, because it is one of the few moments when there is no pain. Happiness has become the absence of pain to someone who has a reality that life is terrible and full of separation and suffering.

With a reality of separation and suffering, life exists for him or her on a scale that goes from minus ten to zero. Life is not a positive experience, it is, at best, a non-negative one.

We plant a little seed of positive energy, but it never grows, because we plant it on barren soil. We plant it in an external garden. We never plant it in the internal garden of ourselves, because in ourselves is the deeply held and unquestioned conviction that life is terrible and full of separation and suffering.

When you are attached to the notion that your well-being is dependent upon some form outside of yourself, the best life ever gets is temporarily better, which condition it is always followed by disillusionment.

Moving Up to Doubt and Confusion

After what you thought for sure was going to work, ultimately doesn't, it leads to confusion and lots of doubt. "I thought this was IT. It was so wonderful. What happened? I thought that if I had this person everything would be better and would stay better. I don't understand. Why me, God?"

It is then we have the awful realization that I call the "fear of worsening."

Fear of Worsening

"I thought this was going to make me happy and it didn't. Now what am I going to do? It is just the same as it always was. Worse! Now there is one less thing that I think will make me happy. I am the same shnook I have always been. It's never going to get any better. It is only going to get worse." Yuck!

We have now come full circle. Now that life is terrible again, we immediately begin to look for another form to make us feel better. The form is different this time, but the outcome is the same. We run like hamsters on this endless track, because we are asking a form to provide something that it is totally incapable of providing.

Not only do we become disillusioned with the form that did not get things to go better; we become disillusioned with whoever told us that it would in the first place. We didn't decide that things would go better with Coke; the commercial said so. We didn't want to go to school, but we were told it would work.

What Do You Really Want, Anyway?

We absolutely do not know what we really want, because we have been conditioned to want what everybody else except us tells us to want.

It started out when our mother told us what she wanted us to want. Our father told us what he wanted us to want. Our grandmother and grandfather did the same thing. The Sunday-school teacher told us what God wanted us to want, and the teacher told us what the principal wanted us to want. Madison Avenue told us to want everything.

Society itself told us what to want. When I was growing up, it was a wife, two and a half children, two cars, and a home in the suburbs. Everyone was telling us what to want and telling us that if we wanted and acquired the right things, we would be happy. Happiness was a function of wanting the right things. And when that did not make us happy, there was always someone who told us that we were unhappy because we wanted the wrong things and that if we would just want what he wanted us to want, we would be happy.

So we end up completely disillusioned with what we thought we wanted and with the people who told us to want it. Now we are feeling like a pawn in a chess game over which we have no control. We absolutely look like a victim; it seems as if there is no way out. But take heart. There is an answer. But there's no hope.

The Only Way Out

There is a way to break the cycle that goes from *no fun* to *hope* to *temporary well-being* to *fear of worsening* and back again. It is this: On some level or another, accept that a transformation is possible for you. Accept that it is possible for you to go beyond the endless cycle of seeking-finding-disillusionment-despair. Accept that transformation is possible—for *you*. There *is* another way to play the game.

Now, telling that to someone is as good as telling someone whose dog has just died to cheer up. It doesn't work. There needs to be something much stronger to break the reality of the cycle of suffering. *The only way out is to be inspired out;* in other words, to have a direct experience of someone who is living from a reality that is outside the *no fun* to *fear of worsening* reality.

Acceptance that transformation is possible for us, occurs when we allow ourselves to experience someone for whom life has transformed, someone who is willing to come from abundance instead of scarcity, from relationship and joy instead of from separation and conflict. In the past, that has been the function of the guru, or master or teacher. Today, there are many people who are functioning at that level in all areas of life and are willing to be a source of inspiration to others.

Essentially, that is what happens in the Actualizations Workshop. People are willing to be a source of inspiration to each other and collectively share a reality of relationship that is senior to each individual's reality of separation and conflict. People become willing and able to inspire each other into transformation.

What Does Transformation Taste Like?

Transformation literally means rising above or going beyond the limits ordinarily imposed by form—transcending form.

We will now define transformation to suit our purposes.

If you took an apple and turned it into an orange, that would not be a transformation; that would be a change. But if you took an apple and turned it into an apple that tasted like an orange, that would be a transformation, because it would have the form of an apple and the essence of an orange. Transformation means housing a different essence in the same form.

To a person who has undergone a transformation, the world is exactly the same as it was before. When you are transformed, the immediate circumstances of your existence are the same. What is altered is how you feel about it. What is altered is your relationship to the things in your life, not the things in your life.

Example: the Transformation of Your Relationship with Fear

The absence of fear is not an option that is available to most people. People are looking for that, but that is just not an option that is available to most people.

The difference between people who are really making it in the world and the people who are not is simple: The people who are making it in the world are making it *and* they have fear. The people who are not making it just have fear. But those of us who are using fear as an excuse not to make it don't know that the people who are making it have fear. We think, "Well, they're different." But they are not. All that is different about them is their response to fear.

If life is the experience of moving along the path toward Godhood, or occupying more and more of the reality of the universe—if that is true, then life is about expansion. Then each step beyond the reality that we occupy, each step beyond the narrowness of the prison of our own personal reality, represents a step into that which is not yet known. So fear is present. Fear is a companion. As a companion, it serves a useful function; it keeps you awake when going to sleep would be catastrophic.

Fear as an adversary, on the other hand, can render you dysfunctional. To go forward we need to make the growth choice. The fear choice is to retreat to comfort and avoid the fear. The growth choice is to take fear as a companion and move ahead. To have a life that is a joyful adventure, we need to be willing to take the risk. Courage is the willingness to be afraid and act anyway. We have no choice in life about whether or not we are going to experience fear, sadness, anger, pain, vulnerability, or anything we consider to be bad. They are a part of the spectrum of emotional experiences of a healthy, inspired person that is functioning joyfully and effectively on the planet. We are not going to abolish those experiences. To the degree we are avoiding them, we are avoiding life itself and we cut ourselves off from the experience of love, joy, strength, or anything we consider to be good.

Our perception is a function of polarity. Without polarity, there can be no perception. If there were no on/offness—no good/badness, happy/sadness—there would be no existence. At least there would be no perception of existence. So on the ashes of our sadness is built the foundation for the pinnacle of our joy.

If we try to avoid the bad stuff, our life becomes determined by what's left after we have avoided all the things we don't want to experience. Then we come up with perfectly valid reasons why we are not doing what we really know we want to do. Instead of actually getting it on in the world, we only think about getting it on in the world.

What seems to happen in the Actualizations Workshop is that people have an opportunity to transform their relationship with those responses or emotions or feelings that they consider to be negative. How they feel about these responses is where they differ. Instead of resisting and avoiding their experience of life, they are able to embrace it. In other words, they go beyond the imprisonment of the form of their experience. It no longer has to be a certain way, it can be the way it is. They stop trying to change their experience, and just experience it. They stop merely living, and come to life.

Getting Detached from Form

The transformation of our experience of life requires that we begin to become detached from form—that we stop pretending or believing that forms will give us something that they simply cannot deliver. That does not mean we need to give everything up. We simply need to recognize the place form should occupy in our life. All form does is to facilitate our being the way we are. It doesn't dictate or direct or cause the way we are.

Take money, for example. By itself, money will not make us happy or unhappy. If you have a lot of money, you can be happy or unhappy with more style than you could if you didn't have money. Money is a facility, not a source of experience.

Becoming detached from form and being willing to experience sadness and other negative emotions seem to go hand in hand. Letting go of the notion that something outside of ourselves is going to make us happy is sometimes a sad experience. Not being willing to be sad about it, keeps our attachment to form in place. The fact that there is no Santa Claus is a truth. It is only sad if we were waiting for him to bring us the gift of a happy ever-after. But after it is sad, it is liberating. Now we can stop waiting around for someone who never was going to show up anyway, and go out and fill our own lives full of joy and satisfaction.

How to Be Committed to Our Own Well-being

Once we give up our attachment to form—once we stop asking things outside of ourselves to give us what they cannot deliver, there is a fundamental shift in our relationship with life. We begin to be committed to our own well-being. We begin to make choices based on the essence of experience, not on form. We begin to make choices in life based upon what will serve us as growing, knowing, awakening beings. We begin to choose advancement instead of avoidance. We make choices that may make us uncomfortable, but we know that they will serve us in an ultimate sense. We simply begin to ask, "Is what I am about to do going to serve my well-being? Is it an advancement or an avoidance?"

It is at this point that life begins to become a positive expression, rather than a non-negative one. We have taken the first steps from a viewpoint of accountability.

A Viewpoint of Accountability

The word accountable is a beautiful word. It comes from a Latin word meaning to stand and be counted. It has its origins in the way voting took place in the Roman Senate. The senators would stand up and cross the floor to be counted for or against a particular issue. It combines responsibility with communication.

The word responsibility, unfortunately, has many negative connotations in our language. Even in the dictionary it carries a connotation of blame, shame, and regret.

Accountable means to stand and be counted as a part, agent, cause, or source of an event or events. So the viewpoint of accountability starts with the recognition that we are the agent, cause, or source of our own experience of well-being or value in life. We come from the point of view of recognizing and communicating the extent to which we are a part, cause, agent, or source of what's happening to us. It also requires that we recognize and acknowledge the extent to which others are a part, cause, agent, or source of—or facilitate and support—our experience of value and well-being.

Accountability looks at causality holistically, seeing all the subtleties of all the relationships and interactions. Being accountable tends to include other realities. Taking responsibility can exclude other realities. One can go from the separation of being a victim to the ultimate separation of what I call the Super Source—where you believe that you alone are creating it all. It puts you ultimately separate.

Often when we get to the level of accountability, we have a tendency to assume accountability for everything about our life that is not working and fail to see that we are also part, agent, cause, or source of everything about our life that does work. It is true, there are a lot of things about us that do not work. And being accountable for those things is a step toward liberation. However, we can become preoccupied with what is wrong with us to the point where our life becomes organized around the handling of our shortcomings. We must be wary of being so engrossed in what is

50

blocking our magnificence that we completely miss the experience that we are magnificent. To be accountable only for what does not work in life is to be overwhelmed with a false sense of our own not-all-rightness.

Wisdom, Humor, and Simplicity

If we move through life in the way we have been discussing, and we assume a viewpoint of accountability for what works and what doesn't work, things begin to happen.

Before this time, we are opposing ourselves, our personal reality is out of alignment with the way things are. Once we are aligned with the truth, with the fundamental reality of the universe, confusion, resistance, and pain give way to wisdom, humor, and simplicity.

To me, wisdom is the experience of being able to live in harmony. It is a reflection of wisdom to live in harmony with the flow of the universe and to somehow integrate the meditation of our life into a social reality that is almost always out of harmony with the flow of the universe.

Along with the wisdom comes a sense of humor and compassion for the infinite capacity we all have to be fools. You might say that we are all latent fools. We have no choice, to be a human being is to be a latent fool. The choice we have is whether or not we are going to be practicing fools.

Simplicity is the experience of unity. There is nothing simpler than oneness. Our complexity is a collection of solutions to a problem—a problem that is only a problem because of a basic misconception we have about who we are. Clear up that misconception—dissolve that illusion of separation—and hopeless complexity becomes absolute simplicity. Out of that simplicity comes clarity.

Clarity

Part of clarity is recognizing with compassion and humor our own process in life. That means to recognize the path before us and the lessons we have yet to learn, and set about learning them. Clarity is also recognizing that this is also true for other people. We have our lessons to learn, and they have theirs.

This one recognition completely transforms relationships. Now instead of our differences being a threat in relationships, we can see that I have my lessons and you have yours. Perhaps you can support me in learning mine, and I can support you in learning yours. Then, interpersonal relationships are about supporting each other's process with joy, humor, love, and compassion. Our relationship becomes a joyful adventure, as does our life.

Out of the experience of clarity, a clarity of your own position in life, come humility and appropriateness. Appropriateness is the art of conducting ourselves graciously in the reality in which we happen to find ourselves, without invalidating our own reality or inflicting our own reality on the surrounding reality.

Mostly what people do in life is try to inflict their reality on everyone else, on the assumption that there is only one reality. If someone has a different reality from ours, one of them has got to be right and one of them has got to be wrong. We don't seem to recognize that we, each of us, see only part of everything and not all of everything.

Clarity has to do with getting some sense of what your position is—what part of everything you've occupied.

Clarity and Relationship

Once we experience clarity, we see our differences as opportunities in relationship rather than as conflicts. We consciously begin to surround ourselves with people who have already learned some of the lessons we have yet to learn.

Normally we never do that. Normally we surround ourselves only with people who hold the same little piece of everything that we hold. We cluster together to support our point of view, thinking that if we can collect enough of the same parts of everything, we can have all of everything. We never seem to recognize that all we have gained by hanging out together is twenty-one of the same pieces to the puzzle, and that most of the other pieces are still missing!

When we begin to operate on the level of clarity, we consciously seek out those who support our process, and we consciously support theirs. Then we are in a position to recognize that if our life is a tribute to scarcity, being with people who live in scarcity is not going to do it for us. We really ought to be with people who live in the reality of abundance. Not to take their abundance away, but to learn the lesson of abundance. Most people who don't have a reality of abundance are so busy resenting those who do, they will never have it, because then they would have to become that which they resent. That of course seems totally unacceptable, because they can't be separate from it any more.

In my own life, I recognize that I did operate from a reality of scarcity, so I consciously sought out those people who operated in harmony with the universe and held a reality of abundance. By osmosis, my own scarcity began to diminish, painlessly.

"I hurt. Therefore, I am." Growth, by the way, does not have to hurt. It often does, but somehow we get to thinking that if we are not in pain, we are not getting value. What makes it hurt is resisting getting it. Getting it is itself painless.

Power

Clarity is power. By clarity I mean clarity of essence, not clarity of form. Clarity of essence leads to clarity of form. When you actualize clarity of essence, what results is a pure form that is of service to ourselves, other people, and the planet.

Power has been greatly misunderstood. In the dictionary, power is defined as the ability to act. It is not good, and it's not bad. It is simply the ability to act. The world is run by people who are effective.

By effective people I mean those who are masters of form. Now, if the mastery of form does not flow out of a mastery of essence—a clarity of essence—then the cost in human suffering is likely to be very great. Witness the course of history thus far. Today, even with the noblest of intentions, technology that is not focused in the light of consciousness will become the source of our destruction rather than serve our continued existence, which was its original purpose.

Effectiveness and power have no virtuous position, just as the truth has no virtuous position. The truth isn't good or bad; it's just the truth. And power is not good or bad; it's just power—the ability to act. And if the ability to act is not focused with a sense of purpose or a sense of spirit, or a sense of service, then it will eliminate the process of living on the planet.

54

If the people who are seeking spiritual enlightenment say that power is bad and effectiveness isn't where it's really at, then, by default, they deliver the planet into the hands of the people who don't give a damn about spiritual evolution and the quality of human experience.

> What is needed in the world is enlightened action. Curiously enough, it seems it is easier to enlighten someone who is powerful than to empower someone who is seeking spiritual enlightenment. As spiritual seekers, we are often ineffective in the world, because we are seeking spiritual enlightenment as our particular version of Santa Claus. It is a grave mistake to make a separation between effectiveness and spiritual realization.

We need power in the world, but we need power that supports, rather than power that destroys. We need creative power, rather than destructive power. But as long as you have people who are preoccupied with protecting themselves from the conflict inherent in the separation they experience, or the conflict they find implied in the separation they experience, then power becomes a degenerative force, not a creative one.

Action—the Tools of Change and Transformation

I remember a man who came up to my office after attending a session intended to help people become clear on the areas of their lives that needed clarity. He announced that he had discovered that he was God.

He sat there with this glazed look on his face and I said, "That's great; I'm really pleased. Now I have a job for you. I will send my secretary across the street to the restaurant and she is going to come back with a lunch consisting of a loaf of bread, a glass of wine, and a fish. What I want you to do is to go to Biafra and straighten things out."

He looked at me as though I was some kind of insensitive monster. But I pointed out to him that it was nice to find you were God, but there was a world out there and results that were of service were an appropriate expression of Godhood.

I often see people get into trips of essence or of abstraction who don't seem to remember that we are in a physical body in a physical universe. And a measurement of our consciousness—the bottom line—is our ability to joyfully produce results in reality that are of service to ourselves, other people, and the planet. It is our relationship with reality and with other people that finally tells us how we are doing.

Often, when I am confronted with taking some course of action, I am reminded of the Mel Brooks film *Blazing Saddles*. There is a scene in which there is about to be a battle, and a Baptist-type preacher is there to bless the occasion. He looks up to heaven and asks, "Dear Lord, are we really doing the right thing, or are we just jerking off?" And I thought that was an appropriate question for someone who was "into" enlightened action to keep asking.

The Ultimate and Only Security We Have

We have always been seeking security in form. We try to capture security by capturing some form or other. We fall in love and are driven to possess that which we love. Our assumption is that possession will insure the permanency of the experience of love. What happens instead is that we begin to protect ourselves from the loss of that which we seek to possess, and our experience of love is destroyed and lost in the process.

We seek security in accumulation and possession. This can never give us security in terms of joyful and satisfying experience. Possession and accumulation cannot guarantee us loving, open, communicative, and mutually supportive relationships. Possessing and accumulating are like buying a theater: you have somewhere to put on the show, but you still don't have a show to put on, you just have some place to stage it.

The only security we have at any moment is our ability to actualize—our ability to make our essence real through action. The only security we can have is the ability to actualize results that are workable in the reality we find ourselves in at any given moment. We will define results that are workable as results that are of joyful service to ourselves, other people, and the planet we share. Once we have come to completely experience that, in any situation, we are able to actualize the essence of our being into workable results, our lives will be free of insecurity.

IV. OUR RELATIONSHIP
WITH OUR PARENTS

OUR RELATIONSHIP
WITH OUR PARENTS

The Mechanics of a Conditioned Reality

Being born was our first experience of separation, and along with that experience came the realization that our survival depended on others. More specifically, our survival depended on Mother. Now the whole process of conditioning begins.

We are taken home from the hospital and put in our crib or bassinet, and if relatives or the next-door neighbors come over, we get picked up and put on display. If we are happy and gurgling, as any good baby should be, then our parents are congratulated on doing a wonderful job.

Other than that, if we are happy nobody takes a lot of notice of us. We soon find that the only reliable way to get attention is to holler at the top of our lungs. If we scream loud enough and kick our feet and wave our arms, then someone will come over and touch our genitals to see if we need a clean diaper. If that's not it, we must be hungry. So somebody will put a breast or a bottle in our mouth. Of course we stop crying, and everyone congratulates himself on making an accurate diagnosis, never stopping to realize that you can't make much noise with a breast or bottle stuffed in your mouth.

If, after the breast or bottle is removed, we begin crying again, it is concluded that we have wind and need to be burped. Then we get taken for a walk and thumped across the back systematically to relieve the wind. Of course we stop crying. We may be crazy by now, but we are not stupid enough to keep crying while we are getting hit. So we get put back down in the crib, and really all we wanted in the first place was to be picked up. But we are beginning to notice what the rules are around here.

The other thing we notice is that we get a lot of attention if we get sick. We get extra cookies and Ovaltine and extra time in bed, and special cuddles and kisses good night, and all sorts of other consideration. We get treated almost like a person when we get sick. Then, what happens to us is classic behavior modification, but in the most insane way. We get positive acknowledgment for negative behavior, and for positive behavior we get no acknowledgment. So we are now headed down the path to insanity.

When we are born, we have a tremendous potential for experience. We have a tremendous potential to respond to our experience in a way that insures the quality of our existence. On arrival, none of this potential is actualized. It has not yet been made real through action. The only thing we know how to do when we are babies is to be ourselves, for no other reason than we just have not yet learned how not to be ourselves.

Now, if you check with the behavioral psychologists, you will find that it is intolerable for us not to be acknowledged, because that is the essence of separation. If you feel acknowledged, then you feel related. If there is no acknowledgment, then there is no experience of relationship, and in the absence of the experience of relationship, what you experience is separation.

The First Event in Our Life

The first event in our life could really be called a non-event. It is this: we do not receive acknowledgment for just being ourselves. In other words, if we just lie there and we're happy and gurgling—if we are just ourselves—then nobody takes any notice of us, for the most part. We have to do something, we have to act, we have to put on a performance, to get any attention. And the performance we get the most reliable acknowledgment for is yelling and screaming or getting sick. That always produces a result.

This discovery is the beginning of our education in how to manipulate the world. It is the beginning of our death as a real person.

So here we are in our crib, getting no attention for being ourselves, and the thought crosses our mind, Gee, just being myself isn't enough. If I am myself, I am obviously not going to make it. If I am just myself, I'm not going to get fed. If I am just myself, I'm not going to get my diaper changed. If I am just myself, nobody is going to take any notice of me. Obviously it does not please them that I am just myself. To get along with them or to please them or to make them happy or have them respond to me in a way in which I feel cared for, I am going to have to come up with a better routine.

We come up with a decision when faced with the event of not getting acknowledged for being ourselves. We decide, Being myself is not enough, or Who I am is not enough.

We should point out here that events are always followed by decisions. We will get very clear as we continue that it is not the events that make us crazy, it is the decisions we make about events. As we shall see, our perception becomes so distorted that we can't even perceive events accurately. So what actually governs the quality of our life is the decisions we make about our perception of events, and our perception is highly inaccurate.

An event is always followed by a decision, and the decision is always followed by a problem. The problem here becomes, What would I have to do to please them? What would I have to do for them to acknowledge me? What would I have to do to get the responses from them that I would like?

The solution is pretty straightforward. We would say, Oh, I know what I have to do, I've got to act in a way that they will acknowledge, or I've got to act in a way that they will be pleased with. But I have got to do something; I'm going to have to perform. I'm going to have to put an act together that will get votes from them.

Here is where we begin to put our act together.

So the whole thing looks like this:

EVENT: The absence of acknowledgment for being ourselves.

DECISION: Being myself is not enough.

PROBLEM: What do I have to do to receive acknowledgment?

SOLUTION: I will try to be who they want me to be; I will do anything that gets some form of acknowledgment; even negative, punitive acknowledgment is better than none at all.

Here lies the catastrophe. We do not know that we got born into a planet for the most part inhabited by a bunch of people who are neurotic lunatics in the area of loving, supportive, growth-producing relationships.

We have no way of knowing that our parents know nothing about being parents. It takes twenty-five years to become a physician or a nuclear physicist or an economist. But we never go to school to learn what it means to be a person, or what it means to be a parent. So most people get married and start families with no other qualification than that they can screw, at least once.

As kids, we don't know that our parents are amateurs at being parents. We don't know that our parents may be hopelessly inadequate as people, let alone parents. So parenthood is about passing along the insanity from parent to child. Of course, we can't blame our parents. Our parents are crazy because their parents were crazy, and their parents before them were crazy as well. Social history is a reflection of the passing of insanity from one generation to another. We seem to learn a great deal in terms of technology, but when it comes to what it means to be people, we learn nothing at all.

So here we are wondering: What have I got to do to make it with them? What can I do to please them? What do I have to do to be all right with them? What do I have to do to get from them the kind of response that allows me to feel good about me?

We have no way of knowing that we may be trying to please a person with whom nobody could make it. It is perfectly possible that our parents themselves were disillusioned people. They may have had us to hold the marriage together. They may have had us out of their own attachment to form, thinking that if they just had a baby, they'd live happily ever after.

So they may be expecting from us that which we could not possibly deliver, and they may be busily resenting us because we aren't delivering it, never recognizing that it is not within the realm of possibility that we could *ever* deliver it.

So here we are in this crazy situation. The only thing we know for sure about our parents is that they know how to survive, for they are living. Our mistake is thinking that because they are living they must know about life. Or because they are living, then where they are at about life is valid and should be copied by us.

So here we are trying desperately to make it with people whom it may be impossible to make it with. We are dealing with people who are subject to their own moods and depressions and elations; on some days it is possible to please them, and on other days it is not.

The Next Event: the Day We Decided We Were Not Okay

The next event, I will call *a significant failure to make it with Them* (whoever They are for you, probably your parents). Here is what goes on: We get no acknowledgment for workable behavior. This is predictable since our parents may have no idea what is workable. (We define workability as something that is a joyful service to ourselves, other people, and the planet.) Our parents may have been incapable of recognizing workable behavior, so we get no acknowledgment.

Remember that the sequence goes EVENT, DECISION, PROBLEM, SOLUTION. So the event is a significant failure to please, and the decision we now make is, "I am not okay." The decision that I am not okay makes the event significant; the event without the decision has no significance. Before, the decision was "Being myself is not enough." This is the second level: "Myself is not okay."

The problem that comes out of the decision that I am not okay is "What do I need to do to be okay?" And the solution is obvious: Fake it; pretend to be okay. Keep working on the perfect act. Develop the perfect set of defenses, to defend ourselves against the pain when somebody seems to indicate to us that we are not okay.

So the whole story looks like this:

EVENT: A significant failure to please or to get acknowledged.
DECISION: I am not okay.
PROBLEM: What do I need to do to be okay?
SOLUTION: Fake it; pretend to be okay.

The Birth of the Act

This solution is fraught with disaster, because an act cannot have a satisfying, joyful, deeply moving, growth-producing, complete relationship with an act. Two acts can entertain each other, amuse each other for a little while, but there is no value or satisfaction in a relationship between acts.

By putting together an act, we have precluded the possibility of ever finding out that the decision we made was insane. If we could have a deeply moving, satisfying, joyful, and supportive relationship, we could experience that we are lovable, capable, and okay. If we could have a relationship with someone who would let us find out that we are all right the way we are, someone with whom we could be exactly how we happen to be, then it would all work out. But that doesn't happen, because the act makes it impossible.

So now that we have our acts, I have good news and I

have bad news. The good news is, the act is definitely an effective form of protection, of armor. Because if we put on our little puppet show for somebody and she doesn't buy it, she isn't rejecting us, she is rejecting our act.

That's the good news. The bad news is horrible. The bad news is, if she loves our act, we don't experience being loved. And that's the best of the bad news; it gets worse: if she really falls in love with the act, we start to be really threatened, if she ever got beyond the act, she would get to who we are afraid we are, which is why we put the act together in the first place, and if she saw that, boy would she be angry! there is no telling what she would do to us if she penetrated the act.

So what you get is the kind of situation that seems to occur most visibly in places like Hollywood. People put together these incredible acts. And the more people love the act, the bigger the threat. So you end up reading about people who seem to have everything in the world committing suicide. And everybody wonders why.

Any act that keeps out the pain also precludes the joy. Acts do not feel, they just act. An act cannot have an experience of life, it can only go through the mechanics of living.

Event Number Three: the Day We Decided We Couldn't Win

The last event was a significant failure to please. This event is just a significant failure. A failure such as the day you come running home from school with all A's on your report card and you run into the kitchen yelling, "Mommy, Mommy, look what I've got!" without noticing that you ran through a puddle and have tracked mud on her carpet. You are holding a report card that says straight A's, and Mommy yells, "Get out of here, you stupid idiot!" A significant failure happens any time we do something that we feel is really an expression of us and it gets stepped upon, rejected, or, worse, ignored.

So the event is a significant failure. The decision we make is simple and devastating: "I cannot win."

Some people decide that they can't win in just certain areas of their lives, and others decide, "When it comes to making a living, I can't win." Or "When it comes to relationships, I can't win." But some people make it a flat decision: "When it comes to life, I can't win."

This decision creates a very interesting problem. Once we make the decision "I can't win," the problem is no longer centered around winning, because the decision has already been made that winning is out of the question.

So now the problem is, "I can't win, but how do I avoid losing?"

Here is the next level of darkness. We can see, if we look, that most of the planet is playing the game from "I can't win, but how do I avoid losing?" Once we have made that decision, the best we can get out of life is nothing. Once we have gotten to the point where we decide, "I can't win, how do I avoid losing?" happiness is when it doesn't hurt. Not bad is the best it gets. We no longer expect it to be good; we just hope it won't be too bad.

How We Solve the Problem of Avoiding Losing

Solution #1—Don't Play

The most obvious way to avoid losing is simply, don't play. If I don't play, I can't lose. That sometimes takes the

67

form of suicide. It is interesting that the purpose of suicide is to survive. Most people don't think of it in those terms, because they think of survival as the continuation of existence. But the word "survive" comes from the French. It is really two words, *sur* and *vivre*. It means to be joyfully and passionately on top of life. But in everyday, protectionist terms it means to successfully avoid being the effect of life. So to avoid losing—to avoid being the effect of life—we may commit suicide. It seems totally crazy, but people really do commit suicide in order to survive. Our "suicide" may take the form of a living death in which we do not participate in life at all.

Solution #2—Keep Others from Winning

In order for me to lose, somebody has to win. If somebody wins, the game is over and I will have lost. So the way to handle that is to make sure nobody wins, so that the game is never over. As long as the game is not over, I have not lost.

We keep others from winning in lots of ways. We are not willing for anyone to be okay with us just the way he is. We are making everything and everybody wrong. We try to come off looking acceptable by demonstrating that every body else is worse than we are. So we play "Here Comes the Judge," putting down other people so that we come off looking okay because we are the least bad.

We see this in business. It is called "Let's be sure the boss doesn't make it." We see it in relationships; it's called "I won't let you make it with me." "I'll change you and perhaps one day if you become like what I tell you to be, you'll be okay."

We see it in other interesting ways. If we hear somebody got a great job or that he won a half million dollars, or someone really succeeded at something, we experience loss. On some emotional level, we feel that his winning took away from us. If somebody we know really starts to do amazingly well, we feel that it takes away from us.

If we hear that somebody is really in love with somebody else, we experience loss. It doesn't matter that we only heard about it third hand and that we don't know either of the people. Anyone who we think has it better than us we view as a threat on some level; we feel as if we are losing and become resentful of "life."

Solution #3—Don't Complete Anything

This one is kind of a variation on Solution #2, of keeping other people from winning. It is based upon the same theory. As long as the game is going on, I haven't lost. As long as I don't complete it, nobody can tell me it's wrong. And it is much less threatening to be kicked in the ass for not completing something than to be kicked in the ass for doing it wrong.

There was a lady in one of the workshops who had never done her homework when she was in school. She just would not do it. She found out in the course of the workshop that she had made the decision that she was stupid. To avoid finding out for sure, one way or the other, that she was stupid, she did not complete anything. She figured that they could make her wrong for not doing her homework, but they could never find out that she was stupid. It is better to be made wrong because you didn't do something than to be made wrong because you can't do something.

Solution #4—Destroy the Game

If I destroy the game before it's over, there are no winners or losers, and so I am protected. You may remember as a child knocking over the Monopoly board "accidentally" when you got up to fetch a drink or go to the bathroom. Look and see today the subtle ways in which you attempt to destroy the games you and others are involved in, so that there are no winners, thereby securing your own avoidance of loss.

Solution #5—Play the Nice-guy Routine

If I am nice enough, no one will tell me I lost. If I am a nice enough person, no one will have the heart to tell me that I am a loser, so I can go on pretending that I haven't lost. If I please people, they will let me play anyway and no one will ever mention that I lost. Isn't that nice?

Solution #6—Become a Problem

If I become a big enough problem, they will have to stop the game to take care of me. If they stop the game, I can't lose. If somebody gets injured on the football field, the game stops, while the team that was losing gets a breather.

Curiously, we have a society in which you can guarantee complete acknowledgment if you become a big enough problem. The solution is called assassinate a President, hold a hostage, kill a couple of people in a motel, or hold out for death by firing squad. In this society, which is a humane society, it is much easier to acquire infamy than fame. It is much easier to get support for horrendously negative behavior than to get support for workable behavior. Terrorists get more acknowledgment than joyists. Joyists get put down: "Well, they are only pretending. Nobody can be that happy." If we can become a big enough problem to this so-

ciety, it will spend millions to take care of us and it will stop
the game to do so. Again, we avoid losing.

So, in the terms of our chart, this is the way it looks:

EVENT: A significant failure.
DECISION: I can't win.
PROBLEM: How do I avoid losing?
SOLUTIONS: #1 Don't play
#2 Keep others from winning
#3 Don't complete anything
#4 Destroy the game
#5 Play the nice-guy routine
#6 Become a problem

It is important to underline here that the events of our life
don't make us crazy. It is the decisions we make about the
events that make us crazy.

In other words, what happened to us did not make us the
way we are. It is the decisions we make about what happened to us that makes us the way we are.

I remember one woman who got up to share in the workshop. She was fifty to sixty pounds overweight. Her story
went like this: When she was a little girl, her mother would
go out and buy chocolates, bring them home, and give her
daughter one piece. Her daughter loved it. "You mustn't
have any more," the mother would say. "Mommy will hide
it." But she doesn't hide it well enough so that her daughter
couldn't find it. So she waits around until her daughter finds
the candy and is sneaking a piece out of the box. Where-
upon she swoops down with a loud, "Aha! I got you!"

So today this woman is a closet eater. She is now pro-
grammed that if somebody catches her having pleasure eating, she is going to get punished. So she always eats when
nobody is around. When she goes out to dinner, all she has is
a thimbleful of grapefruit juice and a lettuce leaf between

two wafers. Everyone thinks she is a saint. But when she is home alone, she goes through the refrigerator like a plague of African locusts.

So here we are going through this lady's story in the workshop and she is in tears. Suddenly another woman starts to cry. I stop and ask her what is going on, and she says, "I have a daughter and I hide the candy, and I get cross with her. I just don't want her to end up fat like that."

I said, "Wait a minute. I want everybody in the room whose mother hid the candy and who punished them when they found it to stand up." Fifty per cent of the people in the room stood up, and only about 20 per cent of them were overweight. One of the people who stood up was as thin as a rail. She said, "My mother used to pull that routine all the time. I just decided that she was an asshole."

So it really isn't what happened to us that made us the way we are. Because if it were, everyone to whom that happened would be hopelessly overweight. What runs our lives is what we decided about what we think happened to us.

Don't Take It Personally

It is getting absolutely clear to me that we do use one another to play parts in each other's soap operas.

A lot of people are beginning to find out that their relationships with their parents were not exactly built on a foundation of sanity. And when you find out how crazily you were brought up, there is a temptation to get resentful about the whole business. That is a great mistake.

We cannot get beyond the mechanics of our conditioning by resenting anyone, because our parents went through the same insanity we did; that is where they learned it.

The shame is that there are so many areas of our lives that are regulated and watched over, and yet this one area goes unregulated. I suppose it is impossible to regulate things like parenthood. But when you stop to think about it, we have to pass a test to get a driver's license, but you don't have to pass any test to become a parent.

In a recent workshop, we were working with a person in the front of the room. This person was a normal-looking, long-haired young man, except for the fact that this man had small breasts and a name tag that said "Jennifer."

Jennifer, it turned out, was several months into a two-year process to change sexes from male to female. He was receiving hormone treatments and therapy. He had not yet undergone any surgery. Jennifer's story is by no means typical, but from it we can all learn a very basic lesson about life.

It emerged that Jennifer's mother was a psychotic schizophrenic, and when he was a baby, she got her kicks out of torturing her son because he happened to be male. His entire childhood was a nightmare of pain, torment, and anguish, dealt out at the hands of this insane woman who loathed and detested all men. As Jennifer told this horror story, it became clear that the pain that he was carrying around was still very present, very real, and held very personally.

The way he had it put together is as follows: "My mother tortured me because I was a boy. If I had been a girl, everything would have been all right. Aha! I should have been a girl. What I have to do to get rid of this pain is to change myself into a woman."

In no way could this solution work, since a change in form, even a complete change in form, from one sex to another, will not change the substance of the pain—and to go through the process and still have the pain would be a greater agony.

I looked up at Jennifer, who had just finished telling us

the whole horrible story and was in the midst of the deepest experience of pain and resentment. I said, "We recognize that your pain is very real for you, Jennifer, and there is something which we can each learn from your experience. It is this: Whatever you went through wasn't personal; it certainly feels very personal, however. Your mother would have done the same exact thing to any boy baby. It just happened to be you."

Everyone in the room got it at the same time Jennifer did. We could see the pain leave his face and the tension go out of his body. It is important to recognize that whatever we have gone through in our lives, whatever injustices we feel have been heaped upon us, whatever we are holding a grudge against life about—none of it is to be taken personally. The same thing would have happened to anyone who was standing there at the same time. You happened to be the one who was standing there. Don't take it personally.

Jennifer, by the way, came to the evening session which is held during the week after the workshop ends. This time his name tag said "John." He shared with the group that he had recognized that he carried his pain around with him to prove that he had been hurt and as a justification for current behavior. Once he discovered that he didn't have to take it personally, he no longer needed to communicate that he had been hurt, so the pain no longer served any purpose.

An Exercise:

Find a quiet place where you can sit and remain undisturbed for some time. Close your eyes and begin to review your childhood. Begin to notice those events during which you felt put down and unacknowledged—look for any events where you felt and decided you "couldn't win."

As you explore these events, examine them for the decisions you made. Did you decide that you must not be okay? In what areas of life did you decide it was impossible for it to turn out for you?

What plans did you make to solve the problems that came out of your decisions? Did you come up with any of the following decisions—all oldies and baddies?

"I'll show them: I'll never love anyone again."

"I'm going to become independent, and I'm going to prove to you all I don't need anyone."

"I'll get sick, maybe even die; then you'll be sorry."

"I am never going to let anyone ever know how I really feel; then no one can ever hurt me."

"I'm not going to play with you [or anyone] any more."

"Everyone is mean and cruel—I'll show them how mean and cruel I can be and they'll be sorry."

As you discover the decisions you made, explore whether any of them are really of service to you in the context of your life today. Do these old decisions support your life's being a joyful adventure, do they support your relationships' being delicious journeys of joy, mutual support, and exhilarating personal expansion that allow you to include more of everything in your personal reality?

If the answer is that they do not, give the decision up: cast them aside, and come and live in this moment. Stop existing on silly rules based upon your old memories.

Also during this exercise, begin to let go of any resentment you hold against your parents; it cannot support you in your life today. Forgive your parents, as they know not what they do, even as their parents did not.

It is time for you to leave home and the conditioning of your childhood. Come forth, and enter into an enlightened relationship with life.

V. THE TRANSFORMATION OF OUR RELATIONSHIP WITH OUR BODY

5. THE TRANSFORMATION OF OUR RELATIONSHIP WITH OUR BODY

Shake Hands with Your Body

I am not a nutritionist, nor am I a body expert, so this chapter is not going to be about the kinds of foods you should eat or about how to take care of your body. The purpose of this chapter is to support you in transforming your relationship with your body, to support you in being committed to your physical well-being. I have discovered in my own life that a commitment to my own spiritual growth and emotional well-being is supported by a commitment to my body. If we don't nurture our body, our evolution as a person is hampered.

Our body is our physical self. It is the instrument with which we are able to experience and express our essence in reality. It is the part of us that is able to carry out the actualization of our dreams.

If our body is the vehicle of our essence, then the efficiency with which the vehicle works determines the level at which our body supports or does not support our opportunity to experience life.

As a vehicle, the human body has had to be virtually indestructible. We ignore it, batter it around, we keep it up late, get it up early, we pour quarts and pounds of the worst kind of fuel into it, then we dress it up in restrictive clothing and run it like crazy. We take much better care of our automobile, which we can trade in, than we do of our body, which we cannot.

Most of us have a relationship with our body in which we experience being separate from it, and we do everything we can to maintain the separation. We keep it drugged, anesthetized, antihistaminized, alcoholized, and filled with whatever else we can stuff into it to keep it from making its presence felt.

As a society, we are overfed and undernourished. The chemicals, poisons, and preservatives that are put into our food to keep it from spoiling in the supermarket, also keep it from being easily broken down by our digestive system, which has the task of making the nutritive value of food available to our bodies. As a result, the food produces toxins, which adversely affect not only our physical well-being but also our emotional and spiritual well-being.

The Secret of Going All the Way

A lot of people make a commitment to their own well-being and find that they can get only so far along in their process. They get it together at some level, but it seems to go no farther. The reason often is that while we can make a commitment to our own well-being, if that commitment does not include a commitment to bringing our own body chemistry into some kind of sensible balance, we are limiting ourselves.

Most people think that if they eat poorly, they will experience the unpleasant side effects at some future time down the road. And that is true. It is also true that there is a short-term, right-now kind of catastrophe that takes place which we somehow miss completely. It is probably the saddest byproduct of all. The short-term, immediate result of being separated from our body is this: The body is an extremely sensitive instrument. It is technology at its highest form. The body is equipped with a highly sophisticated receiving and transmitting capability. When our body chemistry is out of alignment, when we are separated from our body, many of the channels of information that the body could make available to us are shut down and lost to us. And we don't even notice it.

All the signals the body is capable of sending us to help us navigate the waters of our life, all the signals about the world and the universe around us, are lost when we are not in tune with our body.

It is not within the intended scope of this book to tell you what kind of diet to go on, or what kind of fitness program you should follow. I don't pretend to have those kinds of answers for you. I have had some personal experience, however, in transforming my own relationship with my body.

My body and I spent much of our life together separated from each other. There was no relationship there at all. Recently I have begun to explore my body chemistry and to become aware of and appreciate my body for the magnificent opportunity that it provides me. In actualizing my commitment to my physical well-being, I encountered some chuckholes along the path that I would like to tell you about. Maybe it will make your path, which is not always easy, easier.

Don't Make the Trip More Important than the Reason You Took the Trip

I have often seen people decide to get really committed to their body and go off on an extreme nutrition trip or diet trip. And the trip suddenly becomes more important than the original reason for taking the trip—which was to expand their awareness of their body.

So be wary of extreme dietary trips, and dogmatic, "we are the only way to heaven" routines. I have seen too many people "into" certain health regimens who look as if they haunt houses for a living. For example, we can't put an Eastern diet into a Western body and expect it immediately to produce beneficial results. The Oriental body has learned to function on a different kind of fuel than the Western body. It processes fuel differently. To take a diet that has been accepted in the East for thousands of years and to suddenly and rigidly place ourselves on the same diet can have some less than desirable results.

Perhaps we will reach a point in our evolution where we will be beyond considerations of diet, but we aren't there yet. That is something we need to keep in mind. It is no use saying, "Well, Whatshisananda could eat one kernel of millet a week and flourish," as if that means we are supposed to be able to do it too.

The point is, what works for us in our process works for us

in our process. We need to recognize that we are all individuals: our body chemistry is individual. What transforming our relationship with our body entails is becoming attentive and conscious of our own body chemistry and being willing to honor and serve and nurture that.

"Caution: Living May Be Hazardous to Your Health"

If you look hard enough, you can find, among the growing mountain of nutritional literature, that something is grossly wrong with everything. There is nothing we can eat that somebody or other hasn't discovered is hazardous to health. As one nutritionist told me, "It is important to realize that we have never had ideal nutrition, so we can make giant strides forward if we just do a few basic things. Don't eat processed or refined foods, or foods that have a lot of preservatives. Get a working sense about what foods provide what kind of nutrition, so you can eat with a little bit of awareness. Be conscious of the variety of the foods you eat, and take some form of dietary supplement. Just doing that will make an enormous difference in one's experience of his body."

Be Good to Yourself

Altering your relationship to your body, especially doing such things as changing your eating habits, is not often easy. It is especially difficult if we think it will be easy. We need to recognize that if we have been eating poorly all our lives, the sudden decision to change will have repercussions that will have to be dealt with. If, for example, we have been eating meat all our lives, getting our protein from animals, our body is tooled up to process this kind of fuel. When we suddenly change and begin to eat nothing but vegetables, the body needs time to make the transition and to change over from a process that has been going on for almost our whole life.

It is also true that as we explore our dietary habits we may notice that we often eat to suppress our emotion. If we start bringing our diet into alignment with our purpose in life, the emotions we have been suppressing will be released to experience.

Not recognizing these realities before making a commitment to bring our body chemistry to balance can lead to disillusionment and failure.

The Body as a Source of Our Liberation

Beyond the physical aspects we have been talking about, we must also recognize that the body is the place where we store our emotional history. Our unresolved emotions, feelings, and negative energy are stored in our body. That may sound like bad news; actually it's good news, because the body is the gateway to the spirit, to our essence. By working with the body, a skilled and trained body worker can help us journey backward to the source of the decisions that go to make up our mechanical conditioning.

I know a person who was quite certain that her relationship with her parents was complete. She did not think she had anything that was unresolved with her mother and father. She had no sense of unresolved resentment or sorrow or anything like that.

82

One day, while undergoing a body process that involves deep muscle manipulation and stress release, her entire early childhood flooded back. A wave of deep emotion washed over her, and she became aware of the decisions she had made and how those decisions had compacted and affected and influenced her life, and she could see how she had operated off those decisions for a long time. The result was a tremendous sense of freedom and release.

So it is useful to know that in addition to the things we can do for ourselves, such as diet and exercise, there are processes by which other people can support our bodies with results that can be of enormous benefit to our total well-being.

A Final Note About Health

For years we were brought up on the notion that what healthy meant was that you were not sick. Health has never been considered as a positive condition; rather, it has always been held as a non-negative condition. We are discovering that the experience of vibrancy and health goes far beyond the condition of being disease-free. And the infinite possibilities that are available to us as human beings in a human body are just now, after centuries of history, beginning to be discovered and explored.

This approach to health comes from a holistic point of view. Holistic health combines some of the forms and technology developed by Western medicine and applies it with much of the philosophy and viewpoint of traditional Oriental medicine. Western medicine looks at the disease as if it were the real problem. Oriental and holistic medicine look at the disease as a symptom, as evidence of a fundamental imbalance in the system. Rather than just treating the disease, Oriental and holistic practitioners also treat the imbalance and allow the body to heal itself from within.

The benefit of Western medicine is that it buys us time by treating the disease. If in the time we buy from Western medicine we do not correct the imbalance that is the source of the disease, we will just get sick again.

VI. WITHOUT COMMUNICATION, THERE IS NOTHING

In the Bible, they talk about the Word. In the beginning was the Word, and the Word was with God and the Word was God. The Bible tells us that in the Word is the creation of everything.

It is certainly true in the world as we know it. Look around the room you are sitting in. There is nothing that did not get there as a result of communication. There wouldn't be a house if someone did not communicate about houses. We really don't stop to recognize that our reality is constructed out of communication. Without communication, there would be nothing. There isn't anything made that got here by chance. It all required that some form of communication flowed between people.

That's communication at the level of *things*. It is communicating about walls and pipes and electricity. But when it comes to relationships and life, we are looking at communication at a different level.

Communication Is the Basis of Relationship

If we can get that the room wouldn't be here without communication, then we ought to be able to see that relationships would not exist without communication.

Relationships are not about walls and pipes unless you are talking about a working relationship. But the kind of relationship we are talking about is a relationship between people's essences, between each other's spirit. In other words, "I hear who you are and you hear who I am." It requires that we, as the American Indians used to say, "walk a mile in each other's moccasins."

For the most part, our essence is usually buried very deeply beneath the act and the pretenses we have put together. It hardly ever comes up for air. There is rarely a moment when the essence is there to get communicated to. In this chapter, we will look at ways to communicate which allow us to reach each other at the level of essence.

Are You In There?

An enormous part of communication revolves around truly appreciating each other's reality. In other words, to communicate to you, I must have reached you and touched you, and you must have reached and touched me in some way. I can't reach you, nor you me, unless we have an appreciation of each other's personal reality.

Reality

There are always four realities. There is your reality, there is my reality, there is the social reality, which is nothing more than the distillation of all the yous and mes on the planet; then there is the reality of the fundamental nature of the universe. All realities change, except the fundamental reality. That never changes. My notion of successful living is that it is a product of having a personal reality that is in harmony with the fundamental nature of the universe.

Your personal reality is made up of your perceptions of the broader fundamental reality of the universe. And you will perceive part of it, but not all of it.

It is important to see that whatever reality you have is a part of everything, it is not all of everything. Now, if we can recognize that our reality is a part of everything, then we are not separate. If we recognize that it's not all of everything, then we have had the next realization that can lead us to wisdom. Because our reality is part of everything, we can be united; because it is not all of everything, we have the space to grow.

If the fundamental reality were a multicolored ball around which we all are standing, my personal reality would be made up of my perception of the part of the ball I can perceive. So I might have a personal reality that says the ball is mostly red. You may have a personal reality that says the ball is mostly blue. Someone else may say it looks mostly yellow from where he is. Each of us has a part of the whole. None of us has all. But each personal reality adds dimension to what we can experience individually.

Unfortunately, what happens in most cases is that we argue about which reality is "right," which view of the ball is the "correct" view of the ball. We see our differences in reality as a conflict instead of a contribution. We somehow fail to see that your perception of the world adds dimension to my perception of the world.

In relationships, what is more significant than what part of everything you perceive, is the importance you attach to it. First we perceive an event, then we make a decision about it, invent problems about it, and then come up with solutions to the problems. Those solutions in themselves become the source of the next problem.

Our own personal illusion of separation is built out of the differences between the meanings I place on my perceptions of my part of reality, and the meanings you place on your perceptions of reality. For me to communicate to you, I have to be aware of your personal reality.

Let's look at it this way. The spectrum of light goes from infrared at one end to ultraviolet at the other. But you and I can perceive only from red to violet. The two at the ends, infrared and ultraviolet, are not part of the visible spectrum. So the limits of our personal realities are red and violet. If I wanted to communicate "red" to you, I would draw the color red and show it to you. You would say, "Yes, red."

Let's imagine that your range of perception is broader than mine and you are somehow able to see and draw both infrared and ultraviolet. There is no way you can communicate them to me. You can draw infrared and hold it up to me and say, "Stewart, that is what infrared looks like." And I would say, "But I see only a blank page." It simply is not within the realms of my ability to perceive.

I also cannot hear above the sound of twenty thousand cycles. It is impossible for me to hear that on any conscious level. So if you came along and tried to communicate above twenty thousand cycles of sound or the colors of ultraviolet or infrared, you couldn't communicate to me. Not because you couldn't experience them, but because I couldn't. It would be beyond the realms of my perceptions.

To communicate, we need to be aware of the other person's reality and the limits of his abilities in perception.

Imagine each person's reality as a series of concentric circles. The innermost circle is that part of one's reality which he perceives and experiences completely—the part he is aware of and of which he is master. It is the part one knows by direct experience. The next circle would represent the part one has heard about, thought about, and accepted, but hasn't directly perceived or experienced. Whatever exists there, exists only through belief. Then there is the circle that represents what one has heard and read about finds very hard to accept. That is the level of resistance to belief. Out-

BEYOND CURRENT LIMITS OF PERCEPTION

side of that is the rest of the universe, into which one has almost no perception.

If you communicate something that falls outside of a person's circles, he can't hear you. It's like trying to communicate twenty thousand cycles to me; it's like trying to show me infrared. You cannot communicate with somebody unless your communication falls within the concentric circles that make up his personal reality.

Tennis, Anyone?

Imagine that you and I are playing tennis. Also imagine that I am much better than you are. The ball becomes a symbol of communication between us. I hit you easy ones and you hit them back. Simple. But what if I whizzed one by you so fast that it was out of your reality and you didn't even see it go by? If I hit balls like that, it precludes our playing tennis at all.

If I just hit you easy ones, you would get them back, but it would become boring, because you don't have an experience of yourself. You have not had to discover more of yourself by having to expand.

If I hit the balls hard enough so that you can get them back over the net if you extend yourself and expand, then we have growth going on. If I hit it so you can't even see it, nothing happens. If I hit them so you do see them but can never return them, we are not really playing the game called tennis, we are playing "screw you": you will end up feeling unloved and incapable in tennis—and less capable in life. I could also hit the ball just hard enough so that you would have to extend yourself to get it back but you could do it. This is what growth is all about.

How to Listen Loudly

Any exchange between us is a form of communication. Anything that ends up with my having an experience of you and your having an experience of me constitutes communication. At the ultimate level, what happens is I have a complete and total experience of your essence, and you of mine. That's a very spiritual communication between two people.

Fundamentally, communication is the experience of sharing each other's essence through the exploration of each other's reality. The path to each other's essence lies in the exploration of each other's reality. Some of us are highly evolved enough to be able to perceive a person's essence immediately, but that's a little bit boring, because it doesn't leave anything to talk about. Conversation is the vehicle for the exploration of each other's reality. But too often it isn't. Too often it is an argument over somebody else's reality.

Listening is an important part of the Actualizations experience. Out of the forty-eight hours of the workshop, if you spend fifteen minutes of it talking, that's a lot. The rest of the workshop we spend listening—being exposed to the personal realities of ninety-nine other people. Most people can't communicate, because they can't listen. We can't communicate unless we have perceived the other person's reality. And we can't do that while we are talking.

In the normal course of events, we do not listen to discover what the other person's reality is. We only listen to evaluate the rightness or wrongness of the other person's reality compared to our own.

Unless we are willing to fully appreciate the position of

other people, communication will fail. Unless we are willing to have them communicate their reality to us, and not make them wrong, communication will fail.

What passes for communication is really people laying their trips on one another. I will lay my trip, called my personal reality, on you, and you will then lay your trip, called your personal reality, on me. That is called communication. My routine is, my act is more valid than your act. And your routine is, your act is more valid than mine. What we are really doing is trying to hit the tennis ball as hard as we possibly can at each other while saying, "There! Try and get that one back, smart ass!"

Communication is the process of my expanding my reality to include yours, and your expanding your reality to include mine. To communicate, we have got to be able to do that without conflict.

We have got to give up playing the game from the position of "How do I avoid losing?" which is what almost everyone is doing. While you're talking, I'm busily trying to figure out what I am going to say when you've stopped. And when you stop and I start talking, I don't pay any attention to how you're receiving me. I'm too busy trying to figure out how I am going to defend what I am saying when you contradict me or argue with it when I finish.

I never hear you, because I'm inside my head about what I am going to say. I never hear me, because I am too busy worrying how I am going to defend myself when you attack. It is not communication, it is a sword fight. Notice that when someone says something that actually does get through to us, we say, "Touché."

Communication can take place between two people when each of them has expanded their own reality to include the other person's reality without conflict. The truth about you and me is that we have fundamentally similar essences and different realities. The different realities enable the game called relationship to take place. And the experience of the similarity of essence allows the game called relationship to take place without threat. You can have a lot more fun playing the game if you are not worried about the outcome.

What happens in the workshop is that a lot of the threat goes out of people's lives, because they have had a glimpse of other people's essence. They experience the harmony of essences and see the differences in our realities as being opportunities for relationship rather than conflicts between us. They come to see the differences in our realities as the fundamental ingredient in a marvelously exciting adventure called the game of life.

Having touched, experienced, witnessed, and revealed each other's essence, we say, "Wow! At that very deep, fundamental level, we are united, we are the same." And thank goodness for our differences, because without them, what would there be to share? What would there be to explore?

The Art of Disengagement, or How Not to Take Everything Personally

Communication starts with the ability to listen, to listen without judgment. That is what I mean by disengagement—to disengage from our preoccupation with our own reality, to stop seeing other people's reality as the enemy, as a threat to ours. Disengagement means ending the conflict and recognizing that communication does require that we expand our reality to include the other person's reality and that theirs is as much a part of everything as our reality is a part of everything.

Another way of talking about disengagement is to say

don't take everything personally—don't see everything in terms of how it affects you. We cannot start to relate to people, we can't really touch their essence and have them touch ours, until we stop listening to what they are saying in terms of how it affects us and start listening to what they are saying in terms of how it affects them.

Most of the time in life we are no more than extras in other people's soap operas, in the scripting of which we had no part. They are simply using us so that they can continue with the production of the soap opera of their lives. We are the audience for and are the instrument of the dramatization of their act. We simply have the part of extras, and anyone else in their life would be given the same role to play that they had allocated to us.

Our preoccupation with ourselves—our preoccupation that views everything in terms of what it means to or about us—drives us to take everything personally, when in reality other people's reactions to us have nothing personally to do with us and everything to do with where they themselves are coming from.

The way they relate to us, they would relate to anyone who represented to them whatever they have decided we represent to them. NEVER take another person's reaction (bad or good), personally because it comes out of his conditioned reality. It has nothing to do with us.

We keep trying to figure out how to behave based upon the way people relate to our life, not recognizing that the way we see them relating to our life is an illusion. The way they seem to be relating to our life is simply the way in which they relate to their own life, which doesn't have anything to do with us. We just happen to be an extra from central casting. It's nothing personal. To build up our whole system of behavior, to build our whole way of relating based upon people's response to what we think is us, and not to recognize that it's no more than a statement of their response to their own life, is a horrible mistake.

We must disengage ourselves; we must stop taking things personally. We must stop passing all communication through our system to see how we are going to protect ourselves.

Listening for Effects

We need to see people in relation to *their* lives, not in relation to *our* lives. If people's relationships with their own lives are unhappy, then our relationships with them are going to be unhappy as well. It will be impossible for their relationships to our lives to be fulfilling unless their relationships with their own lives are fulfilling.

If your relationship with your life is marvelous, then my relationship with you will be marvelous (provided of course that *I* am not crazy). To the extent that people's relationships with their own lives don't work, it affects all of us. We are like dwellers in a cosmic fishpond, and if we drop a pebble the ripples touch us all. So, part of listening is listening and looking for the effects that people produce around them.

A Sixty-forty Proposition

If people are always saying and doing really nice things, but every time people are around them they go "Yuck!" you can be sure they are communicating something other than what they are saying.

Sixty per cent of what people communicate is not verbal. So, in listening, we can't just listen to the 40 per cent—to what people say. We need to listen to the other 60 per cent— to the effects that they produce around them. So no matter what they are saying, no matter what they say their intentions are, what they are collecting around them in physical reality is the ultimate testimony of where they are, and what is really going on with them.

If a person is being very pleasant on a verbal level and if the people around him are not responding joyfully or are feeling alienated, then you know that 60 per cent of the communication is bad news and the 40 per cent that you can hear is a smoke screen.

Most of the time, our verbal and non-verbal communication to people is in conflict. That renders us very ineffective. It is like when Mother says to Johnny, "My, that's a lovely painting you made." Here's the 40 per cent. The 60 per cent is saying, "Damn it, Johnny, why do you have to bring your stupid picture here when I am fixing dinner; can't you see I am busy?" (Mother has read somewhere that she has to be an accepting mother.) The child gets very confusing messages, because he definitely picks up the 60 per cent. That kind of conflict in our communication destroys our relationship.

In the workshop, people experience communicating very powerfully, because they have an opportunity to bring the 40 per cent and the 60 per cent into alignment. There is no conflict. When there is a conflict between what we say and the results in our life, we experience being ineffective and unlovable.

When we are listening for effects, we are listening for the 60 per cent. The way we know what that is is to look at the results, because the results are the real acknowledgment of the sum total. Results reflect the real operating bases of people—their unspoken underlying personal realities, realities they are probably not aware that they have. If the reality is negative, there will always be negative results.

Listening for Our Own Response

In the workshop, we sometimes use a recording of a wind harp. A wind harp is an instrument that makes a sound when the wind blows through it. When the frequency of the vibration of the wind has a harmonious relationship with the fundamental frequency of the strings of the harp, it resonates and makes a sound. The harp mirrors and is responsive to the charming moods of the wind.

The same thing goes on with us. When we get ourselves out of the way, we receive and resonate with the changing moods and emotions of the people around us.

If we are normally cheerful and happy, and around certain people we feel uptight and angry, it may be that we are picking up the 60 per cent that they are not saying.

Our body is like a radio receiver with an antenna. When we are clear that it is not our own 60 per cent, then we can realize that we are picking up the emotional tone of the persons with us. We are the harp and they are the wind. Recognizing that, allows you to disengage. It allows you to not take things personally. You stop trying to repair yourself, and see where other people are coming from.

Listening for Patterns

Most of us are like juke boxes. Only, we never have any fun with them, because it's the world that puts in the nickel and presses the button. Whenever we experience a certain category of events, we play selection number 73. When we experience another category of events, we will play selection number 57. We treat every situation, every category of events that presents itself to us, as an opportunity to avoid loss. We automatically pull out and play the appropriate response to avoid losing in this particular situation. For example, with members of the opposite sex, we might play our "suave and sophisticated" selection; with our boss, we might play a number that looks like "Mr. Sincere and Dependable." It is all part of the solution to the avoidance of loss.

Listening for Discord

In order to be able really to support people, we need to be willing to listen for the discord, for the discrepancy between their 40 per cent and their 60 per cent. Listening for discord requires that we accurately hear what is going on, both on the surface and underneath, and recognize the discrepancy between them.

If somebody's words are, "It's so nice to see you," and your experience is, "This person wants to get the hell out of here," you can be sure there is a discord. To really recognize what is going on requires that we disengage from the situation.

Too often we will suppress our experience of the discord in somebody else's reality. We don't want to see it. We don't want to be accountable for recognizing where other people are coming from. So, rather than acknowledging that we do see a disharmony, we will turn down our own awareness to match theirs. Then neither one of us can see it.

We suffer for other people. Rather than witness other people's discomfort when we support them by sharing our own experience of discord, we will suppress our own experience, turn down our own consciousness, be nice, and have nothing happen.

If I experience that something is out of harmony in your reality, I will feel bad for you. But I will not allow you to feel bad for yourself. I will suffer for you by protecting you from knowing something that would truly serve you to let go of. Since it is much easier to let go of something once you have a hold on it, you would definitely be served by knowing my experience of the discord in your communication. But we would much rather fool each other and pretend to get away with it than go through the discomfort of telling each other the truth and have our essences serve each other.

We resist serving each other in this way because we are attached to the form of our relationship, and attachment to form precludes any experience of essence.

How Not to Listen

Do not listen to literal meanings. What comes out of people's mouths almost never has anything to do with what is really going on. People will not tell you, in words, where they are, but they will communicate it very loudly. What people are not saying should talk louder than what they say. If you listen to the literal meanings, you will have a life filled with unpleasant surprises.

There are a few people who really are where they say they are and are who they appear to be. Most of us, however, have decided at an early age that saying where we really are is not right for us, because we did it once and it did not work. We fail to recognize that with the person with whom we tried it, nothing would have worked. We need to be aware that some people give us the space to be who we are, and some don't.

On the one hand, Freud said defense mechanisms are necessary and desirable. On the other, the humanistic psychologists say that you shouldn't have any at all. Both positions are inaccurate. There are some people whom you ought to protect yourself from. It is not that they are bad people. Rattlesnakes may not know that they love all living creatures, so if you walk through a field of rattlesnakes who don't know how beautiful they are, you are likely to have an out-of-the-body experience.

People are like that. Until they find out who they are, you had better take precautions to protect yourself from the ill effects of who they're visibly pretending they are. And it's nothing personal.

It helps to recognize that we never really say where it's at for us, as a way of protecting ourselves. If we really want to have a relationship with people, we need to be willing to have them tell us the way it is for them, without judging them or telling them it's all right. We should not do either. We should say, "It is all right with me for you to be where you're at, but let's find out if it's all right with you."

Once again, we are looking to see what their relationship is with their own lives, not with ours. In supporting someone in a relationship, we need to do that which enhances their relationship with their own lives, and only this will enhance the relationship we share.

Most of us never do that. We resonate so rapidly with people that as soon as someone else is low, we come down. So we try to cheer them up, try to change their realities, and we do it not for them but for ourselves—so that we will feel better.

For a relationship to even have a chance of working, we need to be willing and able to let other people own their own experience. Instead of trying to help them out of where they are, we need to support them in moving through it, in learning the lesson that is there to learn.

Listening for Feelings

Once we can let other people own their own experience, we can set aside the literal meanings and listen for feelings.

In the workshop, somebody will be chatting along merrily and happily and I will suddenly say, "What's all the sadness about?"

The response is as if they had just been nailed to the wall, because the emotional state of their underlying realities, their 60 per cent, was communicating sadness. It is almost always true that a nicey-nicey routine is a coverup for sadness. So many people's laughter is a cover for their tears; so many people's anger is a solution to their sadness.

We are always looking for ways to suppress what we consider to be our failures. Along with the problem of "How do I avoid losing?" there comes a whole other category: "When I don't avoid losing, how can I cover it up?" "How can I pretend I didn't lose, so I can laugh about it all?" Or we decide: "I'll show them; I'll never love again!" Being angry is also a good way to suppress the experience that we lost.

People communicate their emotions very loudly. They are revealed in their voices, in their bodies, and certainly in their faces. Our faces are really like the video screens in the airline terminals. They announce the arrival and departure of our spirit from our body, where it is going to and where it's coming from.

Listening for What Is Not Being Said

What people do not say is often communicated more loudly than what they do say. If we just look, we can see it in their bodies, in their faces, in their incomplete sentences, in the innuendoes and all the subtleties that normally go unnoticed.

To really communicate, we have to penetrate beneath that pantomime, beneath that façade, beneath the 40 per cent, and get to what is really going on with people. And often we don't have to search that deeply, because if we look, it is plainly visible even though people will often deny it.

If we listen for omissions, we can start to become aware of people's own biases and viewpoints. You may notice that some people omit saying anything good; everything they say is negative. And some people are always putting themselves down in a subtle way.

If we listen, we can start to be aware that oftentimes people's conversations are biased very heavily in one direction. If that is the case, then what is not being said is probably biased in the other direction; on some level they are trying to balance themselves. For example, if people are overbalanced in the direction of saying how wonderful their life is, how goody-goody it always is, you can probably bet that things are not really that great.

If you listen for what is not being said, you can often see what problem is being solved by what is being said.

We Hear What We Want to Hear, and See What We Want to See

It is important for us to become aware of our own biases. Like everyone else, we will unconsciously select evidence that will support our own view of the world. As we look at and listen to people, we will hear what we want to hear and see what we want to see, all to support our point of view.

So we need to become acutely aware of the biases in our own interpretations of our perceptions and discount them. For example, we may say to ourselves, "Well, I know I always tend to see things as if they are going to be a problem, so I must look beyond that tendency and discount it, and attempt to look at this situation from a balanced viewpoint."

As we look at our own life, as we examine our own unspoken 60 per cent, we begin to discover our own biases, our own opinions about the way the world is. And as we become aware of our biases, we can discount them.

If, as we examine our own 60 per cent, our own biases, opinions, and decisions, we discover that what we are really communicating is: "It won't work"; whatever we perceive, is going to be perceived through the filter that says, "It won't work." We need to be aware of that and to discount it. We need to discipline ourselves not to become trapped in it.

As we become aware of our own biases, we can see exactly how other people hear what they want to hear and see what they want to see.

Think about your FM tuner. It can tune to any station, but when it is tuned to one station, that is all it receives. So if you tune it to a classical-music station, you will get a classical bias. If you tune to a heavy-rock station, you will get a heavy-rock bias. We are kind of like that: our receiving system gets locked onto one frequency. All we ever receive is what's on that one frequency. We never think of tuning across the dial, that there might be other points of view, other stations. Instead we just automatically and unconsciously select the evidence that supports our point of view, the station we are always tuned to.

Passive Listening Won't Work

Listening is an active pastime.

It does not work to think that if we just sat there and listened without searching and exploring, without looking for the way our listening is being tinted, the way our vision is being distorted, we would get an accurate perception. We wouldn't.

Listening is as active as talking. Probably even more active. As you look back over this chapter you will see that there is a lot to do. The consciousness it takes to listen is in itself the discipline that sharpens one's ability to communicate.

When we say "communication" to most people, what they see in their heads is outflow, not inflow. And the truth is that in order for us to communicate, we must first master inflow: we have to be able to tune in and receive accurately.

Toward the end of the workshop, people become very good at communicating, because they've listened for so long that they are aware of the dance of inflow and outflow.

How to Know When You Are Being Heard

When we do talk, most of us have our attention focused inside our own heads instead of where it should be, outside of ourselves. The only way we can possibly know whether we are being heard or not is to look at the people we want to be heard by and notice whether or not they are hearing us.

That sounds simple enough. I mean, if you see them nodding off and checking out, there's a chance that if they are hearing you, they don't like what they are hearing.

To outflow effectively requires that we be always aware of the effects being produced in the environment by the communication we are delivering.

It does not mean that the effects are necessarily what we want or what we expect, or that the effects are even appropriate. But every time words leave our lips, they produce some effect.

Whenever we outflow, we should have some sense of other people's realities, so we can color our delivery to be appropriate—to fall within the concentric rings of their realities.

It may happen that we are in a roomful of people and are outflowing in a happy, joyful, and spirited fashion. What we observe is that people are getting hostile. Because in their personal realities you are not supposed to be happy, and if you are you must be faking it. Life is something to be endured, and the best it can ever be is when it doesn't hurt, and how long before lunch so I can go out and have my six martinis and make it stop hurting? And how dare you stand up there, with no martinis, happy as a pig in shit?

When something like that happens, we need to recognize it and say, "Okay, I am delivering an outflow that is joyful and spirited, and the response I am getting is nothing personal. It's a function of their reality, not mine. I am clear enough to recognize that my position isn't unworkable; theirs is."

Now we have seen their position revealed—now we have seen that their response to joy and spirit and commitment in life is one of irritation and resentment. So now we can talk to them about irritation and resentment, and maybe ask them how their life is going to turn out if their response to joy and spirit is one of antagonism and hostility. And maybe we can end up supporting them in seeing something about themselves, rather than making ourselves wrong for having a workable position.

Each time we outflow, it is an experiment. We won't know what is going to happen until we deliver it and then notice what happened. All action is that way. All of our action is experimental. The only way to know what is going to happen is to do it and to notice what happens.

Most people do not have their attention outside of themselves when they outflow, because they are too busy trying to deliver the performance they've rehearsed. They do their carefully rehearsed routines with no awareness of anybody else. It is amazing how long it takes people to find out that you don't have to rehearse to be yourself.

VII. TRANSFORMING OUR ROMANTIC RELATIONSHIPS

How to Transform Our Romantic Relationships

The thing that seems to hold the most promise for us as far as furnishing us with the ultimate happy ever-after is the perfect relationship.

All of our lives we have been searching for the one thing that will insure the quality of all experience and provide us with a happy ever-after, free of the pain, anguish, and separation we find in the world.

We expect to have absent from the relationship everything we don't like about life. Our expectations have been fed, since we were very small, a diet of Snow Whites, Cinderellas, and fairy godmothers, along with Prince Valiants and the Clark Kent-to-Superman transformation. We grow up believing that someday our Prince (or Princess) will come, and stay forever as we share a state of bliss untouched by the harshness of the realities of the world.

A beautiful dream, an exquisite fantasy; let us now explore the reality. In a romantic relationship, what I really want from you is a more joyful experience of myself. I will say, "I love you," if in your presence I experience myself as a joyful, lovable, and capable person. And this is actually what you want from me.

The Difference Between Being in Love and Falling in It

When we say, "I'm falling in love with you," we are really saying, "I am becoming the effect of you, and it's more fun than being the effect of the dreary stuff I am usually the effect of."

This is a state of temporary well-being. It is the illusion that at last our Prince (or Princess) has arrived and that bliss is just around the corner. It is the period of high hopes. It is the statement that "I am the effect of you at the moment, and things go better with you." We are addicted to this feeling, a temporary feeling of exhilaration, for it looks as if our dreams are about to come true.

We will have a relationship for as long as it takes for me to no longer be in love with you—to no longer be the effect of you. Or vice versa.

I can go from one relationship to another on the basis that we'll have a relationship for as long as things go better with you without my having to do anything. When things stop going better with you, I will go on to the next one. Familiar? Yes. Satisfying? No.

We are always preoccupied with what the relationship is doing for us, not with what we are doing for the relationship. I am not saying that being the effect of somebody in this way is bad or unpleasant. It isn't. It's wonderful. It is opposite from the experience of fear; it is a release. But we should be aware that in a relationship, the effect stage is just that, a stage. It is not a destination, or a way to measure the validity of the relationship.

"You Are I, and I Love Myself"

When we say we are in love with someone, what is happening is that around that person we have an experience of our own essence. And we fall in love with that experience because that experience *is* love.

Unfortunately, we put the cause of the experience over on the other people, rather than recognizing that what we love is ourselves around them. Something about them inspires us out of our act and into a direct experience of our own beauty and our own supportability. We really fall in love with our ultimate self. It is an experience of freedom and release.

If we attribute the cause or source of the experience solely to the presence of the others, we rob ourselves of the possibility of owning our own experience and recognizing our own lovability. We become the effect of the other persons. We cast them in our soap opera, and the possibility of the absence of the experience becomes a threat. Eventually it comes to an end, usually a sad one.

When you give somebody else ownership of your sense of well-being, it can lead only to the deterioration of your well-being. If you think that the experience you have of loving yourself around others comes out of them, you will end up needing them. They will have to be around for you to experience your own true nature.

What you love is your experience of yourself. Don't give credit to the mirror for what you see reflected there.

Being in Love

To me, being in love is experiencing a person's essence and expression of that essence, and being unwilling for the other person not to express it. I love you if I experience your essence and support your expression of your essence and won't allow you to hide the beauty of your real self. The experience of real love exists beyond any considerations we have for our own well-being.

Love is when I am concerned with your relationship with your own life rather than with your relationship to mine. I love you, knowing that if your relationship with yourself works, your relationship with me will automatically work, and if your relationship with yourself and your own life doesn't work, your relationship with me won't work either.

Love is the experience of our unity—the experience that between you and me there is no separation and therefore no conflict. It is the experience that between you and me exists a fundamental harmony and balance in relationship that is an expression of the fundamental nature of the universe.

My observation is that whenever you can get people to be themselves and to express themselves graciously and with an appropriateness that comes out of a perception of the reality they happen to be in, you experience them as lovely people. They experience loving people and they experience being loved. When you are with a group of people who are really able to be themselves and do not play their acts, and do not hide behind their façades, and are not preoccupied with how they are going to avoid losing, you will experience a deeply moving sense of well-being; there is love. I am talking about the kind of people who feel that their lives have already turned out and now it's all a bonus. These are people who really experience a love for others.

When we have the experience of being one with everything, we have that experience of being related to everything. All the separation disappears; all the conflict disappears, and we are left with a sense of fullness, joy, serenity—in short, an experience of love. It is love beyond attachment—what the yogis call the awakening of the fourth chakra.

Love Is Insufficient Grounds for a Relationship

Balance and harmony in relationship is the fundamental nature of the universe. We experience this balance and harmony as love. The experience we call love is the substance of all reality. Everything else is an illusion. Since love is the way it is, if you expanded your consciousness to the level required, you would experience loving everybody. But you wouldn't want to conduct an intimate and romantic relationship with everybody—you can't take that much vitamin E!

But somehow we think that is what we would have to do. If I experience that I love you, then we've got to have a relationship. Because we regard love as an unusual and scarce commodity. We have gotten to the crazy place on this planet where we think that conflict is normal, separation is normal, alienation is normal—that a lifestyle that is generally unsatisfying is normal. The brief moments of exception are this thing called love.

The truth is, love is the normal state, and there are a lot of

exceptions called separation, conflict, and alienation. But to
consider separation, conflict, and alienation as normal is to
condemn humanity to what we have condemned ourselves
to throughout recorded history, a tragedy of endless war
and conflict in which millions suffer and die. Just because
there is a lot of it around, it is crazy to say that it is normal.
If we say that suffering is normal, we have condemned humanity to suffering. We must look at it this way instead: the
beautiful, exquisite exception is normal, and everything else
is an aberration.

*Love is the exquisite exception that is a reflection of what
is normal; what we consider average and mistakenly label as
normal is the abundance of the aberration built upon illu-
sions of separation created by our minds. We are related.*
When we are having a relationship, we are simply doing
something about the fact that we are related. From this experience, we can see that if love is present, and if love is
there when we get all the aberrations cleaned up, then obviously love is insufficient grounds for what we call a
relationship.

If I experience being in love around you, it does not mean
I have to do anything about it. Our craziness is that if we
experience loving someone, we consider it to be such a
scarce experience that we have to race off and say I do, I do,
I do, until death do us part. And before you know it, the rest
of the relationship is about speeding up the until death do
us part.

We have got to grow up when it comes to love. We have
got to see that we do not have to do something with every
person with whom we have that experience. *Once we discover that love is the way it is, we are no longer threatened
by the possibility of the absence of love, because we recognize that the absence of love is no more than an illusion.*
We are so threatened by the absence of love that when

any little bit of it shows its head we yell, "Gimme!" and grab at it with attachment. Attachment destroys the experience of love. If we can recognize that love is simply the way of things, and that it will always be revealed when the clouds of aberration, separation, alienation, and conflict are blown away, then the threat of being without love no longer exists.

I am not personally threatened by being without love. I meet so many people with whom I would enjoy having a relationship, that I sometimes feel swamped by the abundance. The problem is responding appropriately to the reality of abundance, rather than suffering from an illusion of scarcity.

If we experience loving somebody, it is not necessary to begin a "relationship" or run off to the Justice of the Peace. We may say nothing more than "I really love you, and I don't think we ought to do anything about it. I just thought it would be a pity if I experienced loving you and kept it a secret."

If love is not sufficient grounds for what we call a relationship, what is? Let's take a look. There are probably no more manipulative words in the language than "I love you." As a young man, I don't know how many times I said, "I love you," in an effort to persuade a young lady to do something I was certain she wouldn't do if she were in full possession of the facts.

If you look at the history of civilization, you will see that millions of people have died in wars conducted in the name of love—love of God, country, king, motherland, and high ideals. Today we have Protestants and Catholics blowing each other apart in Northern Ireland, all in the name of the love of the same God. It is probably not what God had in mind, but they haven't noticed yet. So the words "I love you" have come to be regarded with such suspicion that some people will no longer say them.

The Difference Between Commitment and Attachment

If our relationship is going to work, there must be a commitment to each other's well-being. Most people who say they have a commitment, don't; they have an attachment. Commitment means "I am going to stick with you and support your experience of well-being." Attachment means "I am stuck without you."

We need to be able to go into a relationship with commitment and without attachment, recognizing that love is not an issue particularly. Love is what will be there once we get everything else working. Once we discover that balance and harmony in relationship is the fundamental nature of the universe, then the absence of love is not such a threat.

What Do We Really Want from Each Other?

What I want in my relationship with you is an experience of myself as a lovable and capable person when I am being myself. Unless I am being myself, I can't have the experience of being lovable and capable. I can't have an experience of being a lovable and capable person when I put my act out there. I may have a lovable and capable act, but if you go for it, I don't have experience of being a lovable and capable person. I am just a bad person with a lovable and capable act. And now the threat is that you'll find out that the lovable and capable act is hiding the horrible me that is really there, and if you ever see that, I'm in big trouble.

All we really want from each other is experience of ourselves as lovable and capable people. We want the experience that we are capable of making some contribution that's of joyful service to ourselves, other people, and the planet that we all share. This is very important to us; it is what we all really want.

The Importance of Equality

In his remarkable and moving *The Prophet*, Kahlil Gibran writes about the paradox between unity and separation. "Let there be spaces in your togetherness," he says, "for the pillars of the temple stand apart. And the oak tree and the cypress grow not in each other's shadow."

It is vital to a relationship that we discover the balance between unity and separation. If we are totally together, we can't experience each other; we can only experience each other if there is separation in the unity. But if the pillars of our temple are not the same height, the roof will slide off, which means there has to be a sense of equality in the relationship.

A relationship that works is built upon a commitment to and an appreciation of each other's process and a recognition of our fundamental equality as beings, regardless of our relative positions and achievements in the process of our evolution.

Too many relationships are built on the Santa Claus syndrome. "I want somebody to take care of me like Mummy never did, and I will go out and make enough money to pay for it." And "I want a Daddy who'll buy me the toys that Daddy never did." Too many relationships are organized to be a convenient way to handle the mechanics of living when they could be organized around the adventure of life. *Love is not about gazing into each other's eyes; it is about, together, gazing out at the world*

The All-important Quantum et Solace

Ian Fleming, who was most well-known for creating the James Bond character, once wrote a beautiful essay on relationships in which he talked about a principle he called *The Quantum et Solace*. The quantum et solace means the amount of well-being in a relationship. Fleming said that as long as two people in a relationship genuinely care about each other's well-being and genuinely want to make a contribution to each other's well-being, the relationship can and will survive anything.

The organizing principle of a relationship should be a commitment to each other's well-being. We should not seek in each other an escape from living and life. We should seek in each other support and companionship, passion and compassion for the adventure, love, and a sense of humor regarding the lessons each of us has to learn and for the revelation of our own foolishness. That is an enormous commitment, but once made and acknowledged, the relationship will survive anything.

The Form Supports the Purpose

Most of us do not realize that the form of our relationship should come out of and support the purpose. Instead, we go into a relationship with a great deal of rigidity about the form it should take. We are really trying to get the relationship to conform to the popularized image of what the perfect, happy-ever-after relationship is supposed to look like. It gets more confusing these days because we have conflicting images. We have on the one hand the *Ms.* magazine image that says, "Women need men like fish need bicycles," and the Playboy/Penthouse/Hustler image that says, "In addition to his fish and his bicycle, a man should have a woman or two lying around the house with their legs open."

We have somehow been conditioned to believe that a relationship should look a certain way for it to bring us the bounty of the happy ever-after. Thus, we are always struggling to get our relationship to match that form, rather than organizing the form to support the purpose of our commitment to each other's well-being. The effort to get our relationship to conform generates the conflict that destroys any chance it may have had of evolving into a form that supports our well-being.

It is as if we plant a rosebush, and when we see thorns, we cut it off because it doesn't look like roses to us, when all we would have to do is to let it grow and we would have roses. We must be willing to let the relationship transcend the limits of form, transcend the imprisonment, the rigidity, the separation, and the conflict that come when we try to put the round peg of relationship into the square hole of form.

A Fundamental Principle of Relationships

Once we realize that what is important in a relationship is the quantum et solace—the commitment to well-being—once we begin to let the form of our relationship evolve to support the purpose, then we can begin to see something else: *Relationships can neither begin nor end; they can only be recognized and altered in form.* Since the fundamental nature of the universe is balance and harmony in relationship, you and I are related whether or not we're doing anything about it. What we call starting a relationship is really doing something about the fact that we are related.

We cannot start a relationship. We can just recognize it and start to do something about it. Now, if it is true that we can't start a relationship, only recognize it, then it is also true that we can never end a relationship. If we stop doing something about the relationship, that does not alter the fact that we are related. Our relationship exists as a fundamental truth of the universe. Relationships cannot be started or ended, only altered in form.

If we could really see the truth of that, all the threat would disappear. I wouldn't have to worry about keeping the relationship from ending. I could stop playing from the fear of losing you. Once we discover that we can't begin relationships or end them, we can begin to allow them to evolve, to assume the form that is necessary to support their purpose.

The Real Purpose of a Relationship

The purpose of the relationship cannot be the relationship itself. The purpose of the relationship can only be the commitment to each other's well-being and companionship in the large adventure of life. If we are not experiencing the adventure of life—if we are not expanding beyond the limits of our own personal reality—then it's not a creative relationship.

Most people's relationships are just a dramatization of solutions to the avoidance of loss. The theory that two people
can protect themselves against life better than one, totally
destroys the possibility of growth in a relationship. If we are
to be vital and growing in a relationship, I have got to support you in your process and you have got to support me in
mine. I have to support you in learning the lessons that are
there for you to learn and you have to do the same for me.
An integral part of that support is to allow me to discover
that just because there is a lesson to learn, that does not
mean I am a bad person. We can both laugh about it; we
can both enjoy the constant revelation of our own foolishness as lessons unfold and the magical adventure of life reveals itself.

We then begin to see that life is experimental. Having a
relationship with someone is experimental. We don't see
that, for the most part. We still want the Sears warranty.
We want to say, "If it doesn't work out, I want that period
of my life cheerfully refunded." Well, it is just not that way.
The only way we are going to see how it's going to turn out
if we have a relationship is to go ahead and have one. Now,
if we don't have a relationship, it won't turn out. If we do, it
either will or it won't.

Where to Begin

Since a relationship is about exploring each other's realities, in the beginning time should be spent listening to one
another's expression of that reality. We should be willing to
express what we really want to the limit we are aware of it.

It's true we want to feel lovable and capable, but what exactly does that look like? We all want that gift, but we have
our personal preferences about the way the gift is wrapped.

So I have to tell you about the kind of gift wrapping I get off on, and you have to tell me the kind of gift wrapping you get off on. If it turns out that we like completely different gift wrappings, and you hate mine and I hate yours, then we should not have a relationship.

In the beginning, we have to sit down and realistically look at what we want, what we are willing to contribute, what our sexual preferences are, what level of commitment we are willing to make, what contribution we can make in the area of living. We have to get the mechanics handled.

Two Halves Make a Quarter

To have a relationship, we need to have mastered our ability to support our own well-being. If I can't support my own well-being, how am I going to support yours? Most relationships are made up of two people who can't individually support their own well-being hoping that together maybe they can make it. That's horrible.

When you multiply one half times another half, you end up with one quarter. It happens mathematically and it happens with people. If two people are having a relationship and both of them are in the fractional area of being a person, if neither of them has a personal reality that includes an experience of his own wholeness, then the product of their coupling will be less than what they individually started with. In other words, the relationship will not produce benefit for them, it will only cost them. It will be a source of discomfort and further disillusionment. It will not add to the quality of their experience; it will detract from it.

Nothing is neutral in the universe. It either contributes or it costs. It is either part of the solution or part of the problem.

It Is Not Nice to Be Needed

Most people's relationships are an expression of need, and they are disasters. No relationship that is built on need will work. A relationship built upon need is a constant attempt to answer the eternal question "How do I avoid losing?" Relationships are not usually based upon jointly and joyfully exploring the marvelous adventure that life has in store. They are based upon a desperate desire to make it through this horrible jungle called the world.

It is not "I want to be with you." It is "I can't make it without you."

It is not "I want to be here, and I want you to be here." It is "I want you to be here, because I need you to be here and I won't make it if you are not here."

Can you feel the difference in your own experience of those two emotional spaces? One is freeing, and the other is binding. One is supportive and the other suppressive. One encourages growth and the other is threatened by it.

Once a relationship is based upon need, it becomes a question of who has more control. More specifically: "How am I going to control the source of the satisfaction of my need?" When that becomes the question, we stop experiencing the other person and begin to think of ways to manipulate and control the source of the satisfaction of our need.

How We Manipulate and Control

Once I come up with the idea that my well-being is dependent on you and you come up with the idea that your well-being is dependent on me, we will then do absolutely *anything* to keep the form of the relationship intact. It is the beginning of suspended animation in relationship.

All possibility for mutual joy and adventure in life is gone. It is replaced by a total fixation on survival in living. We then devise an infinite number of ingenious and destructive ways to manipulate and control the relationship.

We may control the relationship by becoming a big problem; one of us will get sick or lose a job. Or it can be any one of a number of "Stop and help me" routines.

We may control the relationship by not letting the other person ever make it with us. That looks like a game in which the other person is constantly looking for ways to get acknowledged by us and never quite succeeding. We may have kids to bind the relationship together. Kids make good glue, because everybody knows it's a terrible thing to leave your kids.

We have a whole arsenal of weapons to use against each other in the never-ending struggle to keep control of the relationship, everything from money and sex to guilt and shame, all the great stuff that country-and-western songs and soap operas are made of. But I am less interested in the content of the madness than I am in finding a way outward to sanity. And there is a way out.

Surrender

If a relationship is ever going to work in terms of life, in terms of supporting each other's well-being, we must surrender to each other. When you say surrender, people imagine lying flat on their backs with the word "Welcome" stenciled across their chests. But, you will find that the first definition is, to give up possession of or power over.

Thus, surrender in a relationship would mean to give up possession of and power over the other. "Wait a minute! Are you kidding?! That is a horrendous notion to think about. If I don't have possession of you and I don't have power over you, what's going to keep you around?"

Well, we really can't have a joyful relationship until we have removed all the reasons to stick around—all the reasons of need, and of form and of living. We should only stick around if the value is there—if together we enjoy the adventure of life, if we joyfully support and acknowledge each other's process.

In the early days of our culture, it was important to have a husband and wife and a retinue of children to help run the farm and keep off real Indians. But things have changed. At a very deep level, we have failed to notice. We live in a society in which it is relatively easy for the single person to get living handled. At the very least, we should recognize that relationships afford only very marginal benefits in terms of getting the mechanics of living handled.

We should celebrate that. We should stop and have a holiday to acknowledge that as an incredible opportunity. We've got the mechanics of living handled! There are very few people in all of history who could have said that.

We have got living handled; now we'd better find out the purpose. The purpose of getting living handled is to have freedom for the adventure and celebration of life, to have the adventure of experiencing love and passion in our exploration of each other and life. Freedom from concern for the mechanics of living provides us with a greater opportunity to discover, without threat, the fundamental nature of the universe and the perfection of our relationship to it all.

But somehow we have not seen this yet. What it looks like to me is that we get living handled, then muck it up so we can get living handled all over again. We are going to muck it up so we can play again, because we won this one and don't know that there is another game.

Don't Require That Your Partner Be Psychic

We seem to operate from the principle that if they really loved us, they would know what we wanted and they would give it to us without our having to ask. In most relationships, we are two people who individually don't know what we want, expecting the other person, who doesn't know what he wants, to know what we want and give it to us without our asking. This is crazy. Thus, a fundamental component of a relationship is the free communication of wants and desires on all levels.

If You Want Something, Ask

Very few of us can ask for what we want in a joyful and open fashion, and without guilt. How many times when you were a child were you told, "It's rude to ask." It is somehow more polite to wait to be invited. Well, millions of people are still waiting to be invited.

If I bought the notion that it is rude to ask, I am never going to ask. And if I never ask, I probably will never get what I want. My life will be constructed out of what's left after I avoid all the things that I am afraid of. How many of us live this way? If you think it is rude to ask and you feel compelled to ask anyway, you are likely to ask apologetically. Whoever you ask will not feel good about giving you what you asked for.

One of the great keys to joy and happiness and results in life is to develop the ability to ask for what you want in such a manner that people are delighted to give it to you. I know a San Francisco street musician who makes a five-figure income because he knows how to ask for what he wants. He can ask people for money in such a way that they feel good about giving it to him. "If you are worried that the sound of the quarters hitting the guitar case will interfere with the music," he advises the audience that gathers around him, "throw dollar bills; they don't make any noise."

Not only do we need to be able to ask for what we want, we first need to be accountable for being aware of our own wants. Most of us aren't. Most of us have never found out what we want, because all our lives we have chosen what everybody else told us to want. We end up asking for whatever our mother asked our father for.

What we really want, of course, is an experience of ourselves as lovable and capable people, and support and nurturing in the areas of experience that are hidden from us as a result of our conditioning.

How Do I Know if I Can Trust You?

Trust always seems to be an issue in relationships. I would like to propose a different image for the word trust. It is not about knowing that you are going to do good things or bad things; it is simply knowing *what* you are going to do.

Once we are aware of each other's process, we really do know what each of us is going to do in any set of circumstances. You can trust people to be consistent with their conditioning, or consistent with their process. Once we know that, the only surprises we get are pleasant ones. They happen when people suddenly act out of their enlightenment instead of acting out of their conditioning.

For the most part, we can trust ourselves to be consistent with our own processes. You will do what is consistent with your conditioning, and I will do what is consistent with mine. Life takes on a different glow when you really know that. It looks different when there aren't those unpleasant surprises. You know the way I am, and I know the way you are, and the pleasant surprises come when we are not confined by that, when we are not being limited by that.

How to Be Together

One of the things that goes on in most relationships is the attempt to control each other's behavior, especially to control the behavior of our partners when they are not with us. We demand that they be a certain way; we usually demand fidelity, which is foolish and has never worked.

I propose a new kind of agreement. It is this: *When I am not with you, I will conduct my life in a way that supports my ability to be with you when I am with you: when I am not with you, I will not do things that interfere with my ability to be with you when I am with you.*

In other words, when I am not with you, I will conduct myself in the adventure of life in such a way that when I am with you again, the time I was not with you will have become a foundation for a deeper experience of well-being and even more enjoyment when we are together.

We need to recognize that if there are certain lessons that you have to learn, that I am not in a position to support you in learning, you need to be free to go to where you will get that support. A relationship should not suppress our adventure or suppress the speed with which we learn the lessons that are there for us to learn. The relationship should give us the support we require in our own adventure toward Godhood, and a companion to share the adventure with.

We are individuals, and what each of us can do when we are not with each other that will contribute to the quality of our relationship will vary. For example, let's say you have all these sexual fantasies, and where you're coming from with your own set of beliefs and ethics is that it's all right for you to go out and have sex with two men, three women, a squirrel, and an Alsatian dog, as long as everybody has a great time. You are so turned on by that when you come back to your relationship with me that our sexual well-being totally benefits from your adventure. In contrast, I may be the kind of person who, if I went out and did something like that would come back so guilt-ridden, I would be impotent. Our sexual well-being would suffer. So we could both do the same thing and have vastly different results.

If we are going to organize our relationships around value, around support, all of us should conduct our own lives in such a way that we have more ability to be with each other when we are and so that we have more to offer each other. When we are together, we have more of an experience of ourselves to share with each other. Our experience of being apart has totally supported our experience of being together.

One Person Can Transform a Relationship

It would be nice if both people in a relationship could be aware of the principles we have talked about, but it is not necessary. One person can implement what we have discovered here and make it work.

We may find from time to time that we are playing with someone who is not willing to play. Too often we take a dancing partner who just does not want to dance. Now, I think it is true that, at some level, everyone wants to dance. It's just hard to get some people to discover that about themselves. So we need to make sure, when we start a relationship, we are playing with somebody who is a candidate for the game.

If we find that we are having a relationship with somebody who is not a candidate for the game, we need to be willing for the form of the relationship to alter. When that happens, we can maintain our integrity if we conduct ourselves in such a way that we know that we have done absolutely everything we can think of, to the limits of our consciousness, to get it to work out, and it didn't.

It Takes Great Courage to Be a Great Lover

Having a relationship with another person that truly works is a great adventure. To be a great adventurer requires great courage. People who love life, themselves, and each other do have the courage and the passion to make the game worth playing. To really have creative, alive relationships, we have to consciously foster and support that spirit. We require willingness to take action even though we are afraid, the willingness to ask for what we want even if we think our partner may not want to give it to us or will think it's bad, the willingness to manifest the courage, love, and compassion to be where we are, to tell it the way it is, and to be real. Most of all, a great relationship requires quantum et solace—that commitment to each other's well-being.

VIII. TRANSFORMING YOUR RELATIONSHIP WITH YOUR OWN SEXUALITY

Both Men and Women Are People

There has been and still is a lot of conflict and nonsense about what it means to be a man and what it means to be a woman. It seems we fail to notice that we are all people. Some of us have male equipment and some of us have female equipment. Some of us have a predominance of attributes that have historically been described as feminine, and some of us have a predominance of qualities that have historically been described as masculine.

To suppose you can tell a person's nature by noticing her or his equipment is as foolish as supposing that you can tell a book by its cover. We should recognize that male equipment or female equipment is the cover to the book but not really any indication of the content.

We have been sold a bunch of stupidity about what it means to be a man and what it means to be a woman. Men

have been fed drivel about a man being a pioneering, independent, trail-blazing, aggressive go-getter—the Marlboro-
man trip. Women have been fed endless fantasies about
Cinderella, Snow White, and waiting for the handsome
magic Prince—fantasies that men also heard about. Those
were the only two options we were given. One was masculine and one was feminine. And we grew up measuring all
our parts against how we conformed to the popularly held
composite of what it was to be a man or what it was to be a
woman.

The Nonsense We Are Sold About Being a Man

I remember my childhood in the mountains of Australia.
My dad had been an artist, kind of a 1930s bohemian. He
died when I was four. We lived in an adobe hut on three
and a half acres of land in the Blue Mountains of Australia,
sixty miles west of Sydney. We had marvelous fruit trees in
the garden but that was about it. The house itself was built
of bricks made by filling gasoline cans with adobe. The roof
was tin and the walls were plastered inside and out with
adobe. There was a little lake where I used to sail boats, an
outhouse, and a bathtub supplied by a wood-burning water
heater.

We lived pretty much in isolation—a mile and a half from
school or other families with children. We did not have an
automobile and it was a mile walk to the bus. I never really
got on too well with the other children. I just was interested
in other things than they were.

My mother thought I should go to a really "good" school.
I felt I was saved from this unwanted fate because we
couldn't possibly afford a "good" school. I was wrong. My

mother got me to sit still long enough to take an entrance examination for a very *House and Garden* boarding school called Barker College. It was one of the star English-style boarding schools in Australia and had the customary five-year waiting list for entrance. To my horror, as a result of taking the entrance examination I ended up with immediate entrance and a scholarship.

I remember coming down out of the mountains for the first day of boarding school. I found that you were supposed to be interested in academic work of course, but even more important, you were supposed to be interested in cricket (which is like baseball but takes forever to get a result), tennis (we had to get the Davis Cup back from the Americans), swimming (that was our hope for gold medals in the Olympics), football (that made a man out of you and prepared you for other things), boxing (a real man's sport), and gymnastics (for endurance).

I was interested in music, art, cooking, and model airplanes. I was asthmatic and plump. In other words, I was everything you needed to be to be not all right at that boarding school.

Talk about being separate, the only close relationship I had was with the school bully, because I was the resident victim. I went through this for five years. It took me a long time to forgive my mother for "setting me up."

The boys at school called me "Suzy," because they figured I was feminine. Now, Australian men are probably the most grossly male-chauvinistic in the world. There was incredible separation between the sexes in Australia. At the average party, the men all would get down at one end of the room and get drunk, and the women would sit at the other end of the room, have a cup of tea, and talk about knitting and babies.

When I was growing up, the possibility that you were gay was treated with the same warmth as the possibility that you had leprosy. In fact, you could be better off to have leprosy; at least that could be cured.

So the kids used to call me Suzy, and ask me if I was pregnant because I was plump. I lived in terror of growing up and finding out I was gay. As it turned out, I wasn't. I now live in San Francisco, so it would be all right if I were; in fact, it may even be more all right to be gay, but as it turns out, I have a definite sexual preference for women.

I remember standing in front of the mirror when I was a young "man" and trying to think of myself as the Marlboro man. "You have got to be kidding. There ain't no way!" I would say to the image in the mirror. While the experience of growing up was for me very painful, it provided me with an opportunity to become aware of all the propaganda and nonsense we are inundated with regarding what it is to be a man and what it is to be a woman.

I find the image of what it means to be a woman to be equally as unpalatable as the *macho* image of what it means to be a man. The image of a woman sitting at home and making babies and beautiful environments and waiting hand and foot on her Prince is just intolerable bullshit. We have been sold so much propaganda about what it means to be a man and what it means to be a woman that there has come to be an enormous amount of confusion these days over who is supposed to do what and with which and to whom. So much of what we call male-female relationships are not anything more than a pathetic attempt to dramatize the propaganda that has conditioned us and that we have at some level bought and swallowed.

Let's take a look at what traditionally happens between a man and a woman.

Women growing up today can be pretty independent and for the most part be themselves, but when the time comes to have a mate, they are required to turn into fairy princesses.

Men in the company of men can often be toads, but in the company of women, they must become princes.

When we are presented with the possibility of a male-female relationship, instead of being ourselves we go into a complicated mental mechanical exercise in which we try to fool the other persons into thinking that we are the way we think they think we should be. We try to live up to our idea of their idea of what a man is supposed to be like or what a woman is supposed to be like.

So now we can take a look at two people, a man and a woman, who, when they are independent of each other and not trying to relate male to female, are marvelous people with realities that are at least semiworkable. They are experiencing themselves as worthwhile, lovable, and capable on some level and are manifesting some non-dependence. The woman may have a job and be the source of her own financial well-being, so she feels she can dispose of her income in any way she likes.

The man has a job, is responsible for being the source of his own financial well-being and can spend it on what pleases him. In short he doesn't feel that any of his life is mortgaged at this point.

So now the two people meet and they fall in love (a sort of madness, as Plato called it). Each becomes the effect of the other, but an effect that is pleasurable. So they say, "Terrific; it says in the manual that when you feel this way you are supposed to run off together and say I do I do until death do us part."

Things are changing now, but this is still the accepted standard in many parts of the country, and it certainly represents the conditioning we are all a product of.

So they get married, and then what happens? Suddenly the male has to provide for the female, because that is what the male image is about. She has babies, because that is what being a married woman has been about. She has to love, honor, and obey, because that's what it said (now deleted from most marriage ceremonies). Now you are taking a person in the form of a woman who before had some sense of non-dependence and are creating not an illusion but a reality of dependence. And if she happens to have one or two small children, she is definitely dependent on the gracious contribution of her mate.

I remember how I used to resent my role as a man. You know, I was out there busting my ass, having to perform: "I've got to live in the jungle, I've got to kill dragons so I can collect the bounty and put the bounty in the bank so I can pay for the diaper service and the hairdressing and the food and the rent. But," I think to myself with a dogged look, "if I were alone, I wouldn't need a 2,500-square-foot house with five bedrooms and three bathrooms."

Can you see what is happening? We end up resenting each other. Both the male caught in his role and the female caught in hers feel that each other is impinging on their freedom. We therefore feel that we need to protect ourselves from each other.

And that is the way the traditional male-female relationship has been peddled and sold in our society for generations. It is a tribute to our ability to make life difficult. If you really sit down and think about it intellectually, it is true. If you had the job of coming up with a model for a relationship that would make it impossible to be joyfully satisfied, you could hardly do better than the accepted standard relationship we call marriage.

I am not against marriage per se; I am against the roles

we have been assigned to play. Getting married is like being in the school play. We are given the part and we have no option on whether we are going to play it or not. But the school play has an advantage: when it is over, you can go home. With the play we call marriage, you can't go home; you already are home.

If we are even going to come out of the woods of confusion and competition regarding the differences between the sexes, I think it is vital to recognize that men and women are people first, and incidentally male and female. For generations we have used the difference between us as a basis for separation.

We somehow have failed to step back and see our fundamental relationship as human beings, and have been lost in the apparent differences of femaleness and maleness.

How to Get Beyond the Conditioning

Our sexual relationship with one another will not work until we get beyond all the conditioning we have about what it means to be a man and what it means to be a woman.

Women are getting the kind of assistance they need in breaking their own stereotypes. I think that is really what the women's movement has accomplished so far. It has liberated women from the image of what it is to be a woman. The liberation it was originally designed to end was the oppression inflicted upon women by men. But the real contribution of the women's movement has been the liberation of women from the images of what it is to be a woman, and that has really nothing to do with the imprisonment inflicted upon them by men.

There is a definite need for a men's liberation movement. There is a desperate need for men to be free from the imprisonment of trying to live within the confinement of the images about what it means to be a man. Men have got to stop invalidating themselves for not living up to that image. Men really are trapped in the prison of trying to conform to the image of what it means to be a man. They are trying to live up to and dramatize the male image. And it does not work.

Are Women Better than Men?

So why is it that women have seemed to be making more progress toward liberation from conditioning?

For women, the path of liberation looks like an elevation. For a man, the situation is reversed. For a man to get liberated from his image, it appears that he has to give up a position that is senior to that of a woman. This is not really so, but it *appears* to be. It has always been agreed that the man is in the stronger position.

Not only will he have to give up what looks like a senior position, he will also have to find out that he was never really in a senior position at all. For a man to be liberated, he has to first acknowledge that being masculine in terms of being strong, aggressive, independent, powerful, has been an illusion all along, that it was never in fact a reality, and to maintain it represented living in and telling a lie. Men need to recognize and own their beauty, their romanticism, their gentleness, and their vulnerability.

So, for a man to be liberated, it looks as though he's got to take a step down and acknowledge having lived a lie all these years. The benefits for men's liberation look a lot less appealing than the benefits of women's liberation.

Of course, the women's movement is unlikely to succeed in terms that are joyful and satisfying unless men are also liberated from their social conditioning. As women become less attached to their images, the already unworkable position that men are occupying becomes even more untenable. Amid all this insanity, a man tries to have a relationship with a woman. Saying that in this context, it seems, sounds laughable. How will it ever work? There is no way. I have a great respect for humanity for even giving relationships a try. I am convinced that all that allows any of the things we do together to work is that somehow enough of our essence escapes to keep some of our relationships almost together.

What Is This Thing Called Sex?

To begin with, sex is about two bodies joyfully playing together. The mistake we make is inviting our minds to the party. Have you ever listened to your mind while you are in the middle of making love? How can you ever have a good time with that going on? Even though, at the brief moment of orgasm, our mind disappears for an instant of peace, it comes back stronger than ever and gives us a bad time.

So while I feel the potential for sex is a lot deeper, it would be great if we could discover that sex at one level is a non-competitive game between two bodies. For a lot of people, sex is no more than a tennis game. That is okay if it is what you want. The problem is that people do not want to acknowledge that. If they would acknowledge that, they'd be able to enjoy the minutes of pleasure without the following hours of guilt, which may be either conscious or subconscious.

On a deeper level, of course, sex is much more than a tennis game. It is a way of sharing, a way of communicating. It is a physical acknowledgment of no longer being separated. It is a physical expression of unity. Sex can be a way of dissolving the illusion of separation.

Unfortunately, most of us have so many considerations, fears, judgments, and beliefs going on that sex merely adds to the illusion of separation, rather than diminishing it.

Too often we regard sex as a contest of technique, endurance, and frequency. The idea of a contest is somehow implied by the notion that sex is a game. Beyond this we carry around with us a sexually debilitating set of beliefs.

Take some quiet time to yourself. If you meditate, do that for a while. Then start to search your conscious mind for all the beliefs you have about sex, sexuality, yourself as a sexual being, and the sexual sharing of yourself with another. As you find each belief or notion, write it down, no matter how foolish or inconsequential it may seem.

You will begin to reveal to yourself the web of beliefs that limit you in relationship and in your sexual fulfillment. You will, in all probability, discover the extent to which sexuality is a major element in all your relationships, including, of course, those relationships that we have labeled "non-sexual."

Let yourself explore in your imagination your sexual fantasies, and notice the emotional, or feeling, response you have to them. If you have a collection of notions about what a "nice person" does or does not do sexually (as almost all of us do on some level), then as you explore your fantasies and uncover your beliefs, you will be viewing the mechanics of your sexual conflicts and tensions and inhibitions.

In the course of this process, you will start to become more aware of the ways in which you use your sexuality manipulatively and allow yourself to be manipulated by others via the vehicle of sex.

All of this, of course, inhibits the experience of pure joy available in the sharing of yourself sexually with another person. Somehow you have to develop a deep compassion for all aspects of your sexuality. Start to cultivate a point of view from which you can witness with love, humor, and compassion all the sexual actions, non-action, dreams, fantasies, compulsive avoidances, and fears that you have and that another, who may become your sexual partner, will have.

The whole spectrum of sexual vibrations is there for you to be at peace with. Allow yourself to become fully aware of what makes the various parts of your body happy. Become willing to let your partner know what makes the various parts of your body happy. Ask for what you think you want, and make it safe for your partner to ask for what he or she wants. Let the sharing of yourselves as sexual beings be a joyful and creative adventure of discovery.

The obvious advantage of discovering sexual peace and freedom is the joy of sex itself. The most wonderful benefit of finding this peace is that you are a step closer to experiencing yourself and life at a level of consciousness that is love without attachment. This peace takes you closer to a place within yourself that is free from being the effect of your emotions and feelings, your jealousies, resentments, and fears. There is a pure spirit within you that knows the joyful dance of life and recognizes that sexuality is happily a part of the dance.

There was a woman in a workshop who was on what she described as a strictly spiritual path, and very concerned with social causes. She was absolutely against the American system and had decided that life was much better in Communist countries, although she had never been to one.

She presented herself as being supervirtuous and had the opinion that men make whores out of women and that big business makes whores out of everybody. In the same workshop, there happened to be a man who was vice-president of one of *Fortune* magazine's top five hundred corporations, and another man who ran, among other enterprises, a whorehouse. When she found out what these men did, I thought she was going to kill, but she was too virtuous for that. She just sat there hating them.

I had a running battle with her the whole workshop, because it looked as if I were supporting those two men. What she finally came to see was that they had more ability to appreciate people than she did. They had more joys in their lives than she did, and people enjoyed being around them a whole lot more than people enjoyed being around her. They got off on their lives, and she did not get off on hers at all. She found out that these two men had a greater ability and capacity for loving and supporting other people than she did. She did not experience her ability to support other people; she was struggling to support herself. Both of these men knew that they could support themselves, so they were now supporting other people.

The workshop was a totally transforming experience for this woman. When she came in, she looked as if she haunted houses for a living. Now she is happy to be a person who is also a woman. We gave her a sign at the end of the workshop that she said she would hang over her bed. The sign said, "God is alive and well in American big business and in Ed's whorehouse."

Every time she starts to take herself too seriously and condemn herself and everybody else for not measuring up to her standards, she says she looks at the sign and laughs to

remember that there in the workshop were two people with
infinitely more capacity to love and support people than she
had come in with. She discovered that while they were par-
ticipating in life, she had only been hassling about "correct"
living.

Life is a spiritual discipline. And we all live in an ashram
that supports our spiritual growth. The name of the ashram
is planet Earth. You cannot get off the path you are on, because the path is not narrow, it is spherical, it includes the
whole planet. Anywhere you put your foot is where your
path is. Even the idea that you are not on the path is part of
the path.

Whatever is next for you, whatever you are struggling
with right now, is the key to your liberation. Don't resist
your experience. Whatever it is, embrace it.

IX. THE RELATIONSHIPS
WE CALL FRIENDSHIP

THE TRIP WE CALL FRIENDSHIP WE CALL FRIENDSHIP

What Friendship Isn't

What passes for friendship is really a pool of quicksand. For most of us, what we call friendship is accumulating people around us who have the same points of view, the same biases, the same value systems, and the same judgments we have. We choose as friends those people who see what we see and who don't see what we don't see. Friendship gets to be surrounding ourselves with paper-doll cutouts that look like us. As friends, all we ordinarily do is reinforce each other's reality. This is not a great idea, considering the limitations inherent in our realities.

We use our friends as ammunition against the world. We will say things like, "Well I'm not the only one who thinks this way. I asked my friend and he said. . . ." What we are trying to do with our friends is to collect enough evidence to demonstrate that our part of everything is really all of everything. Our friends represent the jury by which we try the world. It is definitely a biased jury and a kangaroo court.

There is no real support in most friendship. There is a lot of comfort, and some warm feeling, but you can get a warm feeling by taking a bath. Friendships often produce temporary well-being, but very few produce value. In fact, our friends can really hold us in place. If we start getting better than them, they really resent it.

Your Enemies Contribute More to You than Your Friends

It is true that people receive more of a contribution from their enemies than from their friends. Your enemies are very quick to point out your stupidities. They do it in a non-supportive way, but if you can get beyond taking it personally and really see it for what it reveals, it actually turns out that this is probably of more service to you than anything your friends have to say.

What Is a True Friendship?

There was a woman in a recent workshop who is an actress. And she related something that her grandfather had told her about friendship. He said, "My dear, when you grow up you will find that ultimately, true friendship laced with a sense of humor is more gratifying than grand passion." True friendship is probably the most valuable relationship you will ever have. Even marriage, or any long-term relationship, must be built on friendship.

A true friend is somebody who supports your being all that you are and won't settle for your being less than that. A true friend is someone who supports you the way you really are and kicks you in the ass when the way you're being represents a lie about the way you really are. A friend supports you in learning the lessons that are there for you to learn and gets you to laugh at yourself when you begin to take it all too seriously. A true friend is someone who helps you to recognize that life is a series of tragic-comic events in which you are not always cast as a principal player. Somehow we forget that sometimes. We always see ourselves as the principal player in our own soap opera, forgetting that oftentimes we are just cast in a supporting role or a walk-on part in someone else's drama.

Whom to Hang Out with

As I look at my own life, I notice that all my friends are people who support my learning the lessons I have to learn. We have consciously chosen each other based on the contribution we can make to each other.

In other words, their reality is more centered and more together in some aspects of life than mine is, and my reality is more evolved than some aspect of theirs. I am thinking of one friend in particular who has mastered money. All his life this man has had a reality of abundance. For a long time that was not true of me. It was just always a struggle to have enough.

Even when I got to the point when by most people's

standards I had enough, I had a reality of scarcity. I would go into a supermarket and get incredibly uptight and frustrated trying to work out whether Hunt's stewed tomatoes were the best value per ounce in the thirty-ounce can or should I get two sixteen-ounce cans of brand X. I would take ten minutes or more to figure that out. Then my friend pointed out that at the amount of money I receive per hour for my work, the time I spent in a supermarket trying to save pennies could generate enough income to buy groceries for a week. So I stopped doing that.

In all my relationships, I consciously select people to relate to who will bring out in me, or support, encourage, inspire, or awaken within me that part of me that needs to come out. For example, I pick playful people because sometimes I tend to be too serious.

I choose to be with people who have a reality of abundance. I won't hang out with people who have a reality of scarcity. I won't hang out around people who have negative energy flows.

Everything I have learned how to do in life I learned by placing myself in the company of masters. Although I read a lot and learned technical things from books, the discovery of a way of being and acting that worked for me and others came as a result of spending time with men and women who acted in the world with excellence, joy, and service.

Being Graciously Uncomfortable

That means that you have to hang out with people who are more awake in many ways than you, which is something not many of us are willing to do. It is often very painful to hang out around truly professional people. Truly professional people are excellent, and when they are doing whatever it is they do excellently, they look as if they are on vacation: it looks effortless. In their presence you can feel like a klutz; you feel like the star of every Polish joke that has ever been told, and yet this is the path to growth.

So most of my life I have consciously placed myself in the presence of people who had qualities that I had not yet developed. For a long time I didn't know how to conduct these relationships as friendships, and I went through feeling guilty about ripping people off. It was not until much later, in my own work with people, that I discovered an important principle: The greatest acknowledgment somebody can make to me is to take what I have of value and use it to support himself in his own process in life. Accepting support from those who are able to support others is a contribution to and an acknowledgment of who they are.

Now I have those people as friends who support that part of me that needs to grow and expand, that needs to become more centered, that needs to alter its reality, and that can be uncomfortable.

One of the things we need to be able to do in order to be with people who really support our process is to be uncomfortable graciously. They won't be upset that we are uncomfortable, only we will. So we need to establish a relationship with our own discomfort that works. People who really learn well, carry their fear and their discomfort graciously. They are willing to apprentice themselves to people and to life.

To keep the balance, we need to have some friends for whom we fill the same function. We have to do something that lets us experience that we can make a contribution. Otherwise we end up feeling that we are not lovable or capable. In a balanced friendship, we provide each other with support for our individual processes; we contribute to each other's path of learning.

What Is a Friend?

To me, a friend is someone who I know will be there when I need him to be there. A friend is somebody who I know, no matter where he is on the planet, has a regard and concern for and a commitment to my well-being. Friendship comes out of appreciation—appreciation of the other person's consciousness and for the style and grace with which he expresses it, and appreciation for the results that are a manifestation of his consciousness.

Friendship is more than the experience of being related. I have that with all people. For me, love is insufficient grounds for a friendship. The grounds have to be a continual appreciation for the other person. There have to be joy, appreciation, and the opportunity to contribute to each other in a balanced, two-way flow.

That is really true for any relationship. It is about recognizing the way in which our processes relate, being aware of what lessons you present an opportunity for me to learn, and what lessons I present for you to learn. The purpose of friendship is to support each other in occupying more and more of reality, in experiencing more of the totality of existence.

An Exercise in Appreciation

So many people in this world are focusing only on what they can criticize, on playing "Here comes de Judge," that we have developed an exercise to help us discipline ourselves day by day to actively appreciate things.

At the end of every day, if we would just sit down with ourselves and make a list of the things we have done that we can appreciate, the universe would shift to support us. We can look at what we don't appreciate about us and what we do, and look at a way to support and expand upon what is, instead of judging and putting it down and worrying about it, and that other debilitating nonsense we go through. It all has to do with developing a relationship of friendship with yourself: appreciating yourself as your friend, appreciating your own consciousness and the particular style and grace with which you express it, and appreciating the results you produce that are a manifestation of your consciousness.

We actually have to take the time to sit down and have a conversation with ourselves and let ourselves know what we appreciate about ourselves. And also we need to forgive ourselves. "These are the things I did today that did not work or were stupid: I forgive myself for throwing the cat through the window. I forgive myself for giving 'the finger' to the person who cut me off on the freeway." Then, after that, actively appreciate the things you did that deserve to be appreciated. Just take stock. Acknowledge what worked in an appreciative way, and acknowledge what did not work in a compassionate way.

Ultimately, you are the best friend you have. Get to know and appreciate the person you have slept with all your life.

X. HOW TO TRANSFORM YOUR RELATIONSHIP WITH YOUR CHILDREN

Children Are People with Small Bodies

Somehow we consider children to be apprentice persons. We look at them as less than people, for some reason. They don't really count; they don't qualify. Our fundamental problem with children is we fail to see what they are: people with small bodies.

The truth is that children are just as intelligent as adult people. In fact, they are often more intelligent, because as we get older, we get less intelligent: the educational process teaches us to be stupid. So, if we are to get anywhere in our relationship with children, we need to alter our thinking about what they are, and realize that they are people and that they happen to have small bodies.

If we don't get in their way, children have a great passion for life, a great passion to manifest their potential for experi-

ence, a great passion to respond to their experience creatively to ensure the quality of their existence. In the beginning, children are just themselves. They don't know any
worse . . . yet. But we soon handle that by laying our trip
on them. We figure, "Here, kid, this trip hasn't worked for
me, so I decided to lay it on you. Maybe you can make it fly.
Here are the keys." It is crazy!

I am amazed at what children are able to understand, and
how perceptive they are. But I am more amazed at how
they are able to survive in spite of us.

The Greatest Contribution You Can Make to Your Child

We are so busy laying our trip on our children that we
overlook the greatest gift we could give: no trip. If we could
simply break the tradition of parenthood, which seems to be
nothing more than passing our insanity and biases along to
our children as our parents passed their insanity and biases
along to us—if we could break that chain, that would be a
contribution that would alter the course of human history.

We pass our insanity and biases on to our children out of
a distorted intention to protect them. We think that somehow we can save them from experiencing the drama of living, when, in reality, there is nothing we can do to keep
them from being knocked around by life and from forming
their own insane decisions about the way things are. We are
not going to be able to keep children from acquiring their
own biases. What we *can* do is get our own biases out of the
way, and hope to dismantle theirs as we see them forming.

The greatest contribution we can make to our children is

to learn the lessons *we* have to learn—become clear ourselves about our relationship with the part of everything
that *we* can perceive. And to provide a supportive environment that allows children to discover for themselves that
their reality is part of everything but not all of everything. A
family is a social reality. It should be a social reality that
supports children in finding a personal reality that is aligned
with the fundamental reality of the universe.

The Vital Art of Acknowledgment

We need to support the natural curiosity of children—
their spirit of adventure. And we need to be very aware of
the consequences of acknowledgment. Our discussion earlier
of the mechanics of conditioning showed the important part
that acknowledgment plays in the way we form our personal
reality.

Are we giving positive acknowledgment for behavior that
is a product of negative energy flows? In other words, are
we teaching them to handle life by getting sick when it gets
tough? Are we failing to acknowledge them when they
relate or behave in a way that truly works? Or is our main
acknowledgment simply yelling at them when they do
things that irritate us?

When we relate to our children, if we are not giving them
the kind of acknowledgment that supports the continual discovery and expression of their true essence, we are conditioning them to do things that don't work, we are conditioning them to become unreal, manipulative people.

We need to make sure that our 60 per cent unspoken communication and our 40 per cent verbal communication are in

alignment—that what we are saying is not denied by what we are not saying in our communication with our children. We need to relate to our children as people and tell them the way things really are.

"They're Only Children"

What I see many of us want from our children is for them not to be a problem. We call it being well behaved. Well, for the most part, the way we see that children can cease being a problem is by being dead but still moving. When you stop to think about it, the adage that children should be seen and not heard is incredibly suppressive. We live in a society that is populated by adults who were told as children, "Sit down and shut up" and "You should be ashamed of yourself" and "What's the matter with you, anyway?"

We still think that if a child comes up with anything, it can't be valid. "After all, they are only children." It is bigotry of the worst kind—it is prejudice against our own young. And worst of all, we completely eliminate the possibility of allowing our children the experience of making a contribution. "I mean, what can they give, they are just children." We teach them that they are unable, that they are helpless, that they are dependent, and because they are brilliant, they catch on fast.

Take the Time to Listen

I really enjoy being invited to speak at high schools. When you start to talk about what it means to be a person, young people really listen. I find that the most frequent topic of conversation among fifteen- and sixteen-year-olds, if you can really get them to open up, is their concern for whether or not their parents are going to make it. The parents are sitting home worrying about whether or not the kids are going to make it, and the kids are at school talking to me about whether their parents are going to make it. And having seen some of their parents, they should be concerned!

My son Paul is now eleven. All the tests say that Paul is exceptional. But I don't think he is more exceptional than any other child. I think he has just had a chance to express it. I know that for the first five or six years of his life, I was everything you needed to be not okay as a parent. Since I turned that around, we have an incredibly rewarding relationship.

We were having dinner together one evening and I asked, "Paul, how is school going?"

He said, "It's going okay."

"What are you into?"

"We're into science now, and I am going through the MGM program."

"What is MGM?"

"It's a program for mentally gifted minors."

"I hope you don't take that title as meaning you are anything unusual? You aren't taking yourself too seriously?"

"Oh, no. Of course not."

Then he showed me some of the mathematics he was doing. I could not even begin to follow it.

I said, "It looks like they are really teaching you a lot of good stuff at school."

"Yea, they are," he said. "But you know what, Dad? It's all kind of technical stuff, it's all sort of mechanical. You know the one thing they don't teach us at school?"

"What, Paul?"

"They don't teach us anything about being a person."

"Do you think that is important?"

"Of course. If you grow up without finding out what it means to be a person, life is going to be really bad." He thought a moment and then added, "And Dad, if they did want to teach you what it meant to be a person, where would they find anybody to teach you?"

I couldn't answer that. I have been trying to get people to hear this for a long time. That basic problem in our culture is that nowhere are you taught what being a person is all about, and there is no source of accurate information if you did want to learn. Here is an eleven-year-old "child" who figures out the real problem in education.

Young people are really able to operate at a level that we don't give them credit for, and for which we don't acknowledge them.

Children Can Be Our Teachers

One evening, I went to talk with Jann, Paul's mother; currently our relationship no longer has the form called marriage. I gave her some news that was upsetting to her and she started to cry. Paul came into the kitchen and said, "What's the matter, Mommy?"

I said, "Oh, it's nothing. Mommy had a bad day at work."

Paul looked at me and said, "Daddy, bullshit. You don't have to bullshit me. If you do, your credibility with me is going to suffer." He continued, "My relationship with you is really important to me, and I don't want it to suffer because you lied to me. That is not necessary. I can handle you telling me the truth."

I felt as if I had been nailed to the wall. I followed after him and with tears in my eyes said, "Paul, I really want to thank you for being straight with me."

He said, "Daddy, I really like you a lot. When you were in Australia, I used to think you were a real chump, but since we've been in America, I really like you a lot. What I really like about our relationship is that you treat me like a person. I really appreciate that. It's not this father-and-son nonsense that they've got on television. I like to talk person to person with you, because I think we can really play it straight with one another." This is an eleven-year-old person telling me all this; I could have this conversation with a forty- or fifty-year-old in the workshop.

If we are willing to listen and to learn, children can teach us a lot about being a person. They are really aware of our shortcomings, of our Achilles' heels. They see our inconsistencies and are willing to tell us—if we are willing to listen.

Children can really understand that some things work and some things don't work. It would be nice if we could stop talking to children in terms of Good and Bad. The notion of Good and Bad is one of the most devastating biases we pass along. Most of the time when they see us, they don't think in terms of here comes Mother or here comes Father; it is "Uh oh, here comes the judge." We teach them to pass judgment on everything.

The Greatest Gift You Can Give Your Children

For the most part, children don't have anything invested in the way they are. Life is still an adventure to them; it's all

a learning process. They have not spent years making themselves right and defending their position. As a result they
can get on and off of a position very fast.

Your children want it to work, and they want it as much
as you do, maybe even more. They can really get behind
what works. And *the greatest gift we can give our children
is to allow them to discover that what they are works.* If you
can support a child in finding out that all he has to be is
himself—that what he is is enough, you have given him the
greatest gift of all.

If children can discover ways of expressing themselves
and being themselves and telling others the way it is for
them—if they can find out that all of this works—then they
can discover that they don't have to put together an act to
please the world. You have given something precious to
them, and to everyone else. A person without an act is a gift
to the world.

I have told my son Paul, "You don't have to be anything
to please me other than to be yourself, and really have a
relationship with yourself that you get off on. If you are
happy with you, if your relationship with your life works,
then your relationship with me will work." Please notice
that that is different from the parroty claptrap we repeat
without experiencing: "Mommy and Daddy just want you to
be happy!" That's bullshit. Because, at the same time,
Mommy and Daddy are saying, "And we know exactly what
you should do to be happy. Do this, or be this, or have this."
We always end up laying our reality on them, and we don't
have to do that.

Your children's relationship with you is the foundation of
their entire lives. If you really support their process, they
will find what's right for them. If you can allow them to discover that they don't have to play from the point of view of

"How do I avoid losing?" if you can relate to them in a way in which they don't have to decide "I can't win," they may actually have a chance to make it as human beings, and we all may have a chance to make it as a species.

How to Support Your Children

I know that I was a very poor parent for the first six years of my son's life. During that time, I left him no choice but to have to play the game from "How do I avoid losing?" But, once I turned around, he dropped that immediately. Children usually make all their basic decisions about life by the time they are about seven years old. But they don't consolidate their particular versions of "How do I avoid losing?" until they are around thirteen or fourteen. The years in between are the experimental years; they are also the years when it is easy to give up all the stuff that does not allow a joyful, satisfying experience in life.

As a parent, you need to let your children go through whatever it is they go through for the first four, five, six, or seven years. It is not until you can really start to communicate to them, and they are able to begin to look at their own process, that you can start to help them dismantle whatever decisions they have made.

Even if you conduct yourself as a perfect parent during the early years, nothing is going to stop them from making crazy decisions about their position in life. During that time, you are fairly free to explore what being a parent is about with immunity, barring horrendous psychoses on your part, of course. In other words, you can be your basic inadequate parent for the first four or five years. It is during the time from seven to fourteen that children can become persons. It is up to us to support them in finding out what that means.

Acknowledgment Works

I travel a lot, so I don't often get a chance to spend time with my son. I call up and talk to him; and he is genuinely pleased to hear from me. He doesn't lay any of that stuff on me about not being around enough. He appreciates me because he can see that my life works. And that is more important to him than whether or not I am around. I am always very careful to acknowledge him clearly when he does something that works, and if he does something that does not work, I don't make a big deal about it.

If you notice, people get very strange when you acknowledge them for something. They get embarrassed or blush. I am reminded of the evening that Carol, a friend, and I were in one of San Francisco's finest health-food restaurants. A very attractive woman who works there came over to our table. She had the most incredible olive skin, tawny blond hair, and blue eyes. She was wearing a blue dress in which she looked beautiful. I said to her, "You really look attractive in that dress; it suits you."

She said, all flustered, "Oh, it's just an old dress that I picked up out of the corner, and I should have washed it and pressed it. It looks terrible!" And I thought, "I was just sitting here eating my carrot cake!"

So the game became one of trying to get this lady to accept an acknowledgment graciously. Well, I think it took us three weeks, ten slices of carrot cake, umpteen dollars, and a few pounds in excess weight before finally one evening when I said, "Nancy, you look lovely this evening," and she said, "Thank you."

If you look back at how often and for what we got acknowledged when we were children, we can see why we all seem to have what a friend of mine calls the "Lone Ranger complex"—why we would rather be riding off alone into the sunset yelling at the top of our lungs than experiencing anyone acknowledging us for who we are or what we did. How many times did Mommy say, "That is a lovely picture" with the verbal 40 per cent, when the non-verbal 60 per cent was saying, "Will you get the hell out of here, can't you see I'm busy?" And the only other time we get acknowledged, we get taken in. Like this: "Oh, you're such a nice boy. Would you do the dishes for Mommy?" So we learn that if we accept acknowledgment, we are going to get screwed.

Some Rules of Acknowledgment

You cannot acknowledge somebody for something they do not experience as real. With the young lady at the restaurant, she had to accept that she really *was* attractive before she could graciously and joyfully respond to my statement "You're really attractive." So it is with our children; we need to make sure that they experience that they in fact did do what we are acknowledging them for.

The other side is also true: acknowledgment will be hollow to a child unless he experiences that *we* experience that he did what he is being acknowledged for. It is not enough to merely say, "That's a very nice picture" and turn to continue making dinner. Unless the child experiences that you are sincerely interested and understand what you are acknowledging, the gesture will be empty and you will likely damage your credibility with the child.

So go beyond the pat-on-the-head acknowledgment. "I think it's a wonderful picture. What do you think of your picture?" "Well," says the child, "I think it is okay, but people don't really look like that." And we say, "Well, some people may look like that. Is that the way you feel about people? If you do, then that is the way they look to you, so that's all right to draw them that way." It is important to explore with the child each offering he puts out into the world, to see it as an expression of his personal reality, and to appreciate it as such. Each offering is sacred and is an opportunity to allow the child to experience that he or she is lovable and capable.

One of the qualities I appreciate about my son Paul is that he is not waiting for Santa Claus. He is clear that it will turn out any way he makes it turn out. I will support his getting it to turn out the way he wants it to turn out. He knows that I want him to get it to turn out the way he wants it to, not the way I want it to. He is clear that he does not have to measure up to my or his mother's standards. We support him in expressing himself. Our measurement is the quality of his relationship with himself and the quality of his relationship with his life. We talk to him about the principles of conducting himself in a way that joyfully supports himself, other people, and the planet. He is clear that he can't set aside his own interests from those of others who share the planet with him.

Everything that works in relationship with people we call adults, will work in relationship with people we call children. And everything we do that doesn't work in our relationship with adults, will also not work in our relationship with children. In fact children often know more about people than we do, for they may have not succumbed to the process of conditioning that leaves them experientially de-habilitated, to function as a manipulative personality and as yet another member of the living dead. Let them awaken the child within you, and together with them celebrate life!

XI. RELATIONSHIP WITH THE BOSS

Enlightenment in Business

How to be a boss and make it work for everybody.

The Challenge of Enlightened Management

If people are going to grow, they have to be engaged in some kind of game together. They cannot grow in isolation. A business organization can provide the ideal game—the perfect environment in which to grow people.

Businesses have gotten a lot of bad press over the years to the effect that they have exploited and dehumanized people, and surely that has happened. But it would be a pity to dismiss the form called a business organization because some people have misused the form.

The greatest opportunity we have in this culture is to evolve a business form that truly supports the well-being of those who participate in it, and at the same time to make a real contribution to the planet. In fact, if we don't do that, we will not make it. It is the challenge of enlightened management.

What Is Enlightened Management?

Enlightened management is management that is joyfully of service to everyone and the planet. Enlightened management provides a game that supports the growth and well-being of all its players and at the same time produces a result that is of service to everyone and the planet.

It is possible to create a business organization that is capable of providing that kind of support. But as we look out at the world, we see something entirely different. What we see today is a game in which the employees and the boss are both preoccupied with avoiding losing, so we end up with a situation in which everyone loses. Labor is looking for evidence to support how bad management is, and management is looking for evidence to support how bad labor is. If they persist in that, the system itself will break down, and that would have very painful repercussions for all of us. The system does need to transform. But thinking that it must break down first is a serious mistake. It is possible for the system to simply transform.

The Greatest Opportunity There Is

Being a boss is an incredible opportunity to get people to play a game together in which they can experience that they are lovable and capable. It is an opportunity to create a situation in which people can experience being a part of a family or a group that really works, where they can experience growing and expanding, being supported and acknowledged, and making a contribution that makes a difference.

Business can provide an arena in which people can experience their own qualities of personal excellence and find out that they can do more today than they experienced they could do yesterday.

Transforming a Business: Where to Start

When Actualizations works with a business organization, we start with the recognition that the business is a game. Then we get all the players on the field together and ask, "Does anybody know for sure what the game is?"

In most businesses, there are people sitting in the middle of a football field playing tiddlywinks while the football game is in progress, and they can't understand why they get the wind kicked out of them. They don't understand that if you're in the middle of the football field while people are playing football and you are not moving, they are likely to think you are the ball.

So what we do is find out if anyone knows for certain what the game is. Now, if it turns out that there is a great deal of confusion about what the game is or what the rules are, we are not going to get very far in playing. It would be like having hockey, football, basketball, baseball, croquet, and polo players on the same field chasing the same ball. If you look at a lot of organizations, that is what appears to be happening.

So first we need to define the game and the rules. That means to get absolutely clear on what the objective of the game is. In football, the objective of the game is for our team to get the ball from our end of the field to the other end, while the purpose of the other team is to make sure that we don't.

Intellectually, that sounds pretty stupid. But, intellectually, most games sound stupid. Take golf, for example. Intellectually, golf is about taking a little ball, which isn't even round to begin with—it has deformities, pimples, all over it—balancing it on a miniature ice-cream cone, and proceeding to try to get it into a hole, about four inches in diameter, in the middle of a green lawn 150 yards away, by beating it with a crooked stick. Not only that, but the person who has the most fun whipping the ball loses, because you are supposed to hit it the least number of times to get it into the hole. To play the game of golf, you have to make that little hole the most important hole on the whole planet. Yet golf is always a challenge, because it's got the one thing that makes it a great game. It is never over. Golf is never over until you consistently turn in a score of eighteen. When you do that, nobody will play with you. But until you do that, golf will allow you day by day by day to experience where you are within the game. A game does not have to be "sensible" to provide value in human terms.

The Second Step: "Who Wants to Play?"

Once we determine what the game is, we now have to ask the question, "Who wants to play?" Some people may not have known what the game was, and now that they do, don't want to play. Or some people may have been under the impression they were playing a different game. In any case, the purpose of this second step is to end up with only those players on the field who know exactly what the game is and who really want to play.

For the people who find out that they do not want to play, we don't pretend that this is the best or the only game to play. We take the time to support them in finding another game which better suits them and at which they will be happier.

The Third Step: "What Can We Give Each Other?"

Now that we have the players and the game, we need to get specific: What can the game contribute to you? And what can you contribute to the game? All relationships are a two-way flow. There simply is no other way you can have the experience of being lovable and capable other than by contributing and being contributed to. *As you experience being contributed to, you experience being loved. As you experience contributing, you experience being capable.*

We simply cannot run a relationship with a deficit of contribution. If I contribute to you, you will feel loved. But if you don't get a chance to experience making a contribution of your own to me, you will begin to feel less worthwhile and therefore less lovable. You will begin to experience being less than capable. And in the exchange, or lack of it, you will end up having to make me less, you will have to put me down, to balance your own feeling of inadequacy.

For the most part, people do not experience that they are capable. They are so preoccupied with what they are going to get out of a relationship that the flow is unbalanced. Then they begin to feel guilty about what it is that they do get out of it. On the one hand, they worry about getting enough, and on the other hand, they feel guilty about what they do get. They do not experience that they made a contribution that warrants what they are trying to get out of the relationship.

If, however, you contribute to me and I contribute to you, then we have true electricity: a flow of energy that builds as we pass it back and forth. Soon we are both experiencing making a contribution beyond that which we thought we could ever make. With the support of an enlightened business organization, people get to have the most wonderful and joyful revelations regarding what it is they can actually contribute. And, for some people, finding out that they can contribute *anything* is a liberating revelation.

The Final Step: Getting On with It

Once we know what each player wants to give and get from the game, we can assign positions. Then we make sure that everybody is clear that we are making the game up— that all the importances come from us, not from outside of us. And that when the game starts, we will play as if it meant the world. If it is appropriate, we appoint a referee (usually the boss can assume this position) and a captain, and we get on with the game.

As the game goes on, we make sure that we keep ourselves clear about what the game is, that it is a game, and that we made it up. We also are certain that we check on a regular basis to see that people are receiving the contribution they want to receive and are making the contribution they want to make. We make adjustments appropriate to the game. Sometimes we find people who don't want to play, and we support them in leaving. Some people are really getting off on the game and want to bring other people to play. Everything works as long as we keep the communication in.

A Case History

The first organization for which we did a special Actualizations workshop was a real estate firm run by three energetic young partners. They were doing all right before we worked with them. After we worked with them, their gross sales went up 300 per cent in three months. The year following the workshop, each of the partners made a million dollars after taxes. Even more important, but less measurable, was the expansion in joy and happiness experienced by the people who played the game with them.

We did not teach the players anything about being real estate sales people. We didn't teach them anything about being developers or speculators, either. We don't know very much about that sort of thing. What we did do was to look within the organization to seek out areas of conflict and counterproductivity.

It turned out that the game had a very clear purpose, which we discovered together. The purpose of this particular organization was to create and play satisfying games that would allow each of the players to transcend the barriers of financial consideration. They all got clear together that the primary purpose of the organization was not to sell real es-

177

tate but to create and play games together that allowed the players to rise above economic considerations in life. This had nothing to do with real estate. They decided that real estate offered the best opportunity to realize their purpose. Financial independence was the essence, selling real estate was the form.

So everyone got to see whether that was the game he or she wanted to play. A couple of people saw that it was not, and they were supported in finding some other game to play. Now we had an organization in which everybody was aligned. All the conflict, all the separation, all the unpleasantness that comes from the dissatisfaction of being at cross purposes were gone. All the energy that was usually taken up with bickering and conflict was now available to the players to play the game.

Every time you remove and dissolve the illusion of conflict and dissolve the experience of separation, revealing the experience of unity, production goes up. It is the same principle as magnetism. When you magnetize a bar of iron, you get all the iron particles in alignment. When the people in an organization are aligned, they get magnetic and very powerful.

The Actualizations Staff

One of the important things a boss has to keep in mind is that nobody can make it without having the support of the team. The boss can't make it if he doesn't have the support of the team, and neither can any member of the team.

In our own organization, nobody succeeds on staff without having the support and respect of the staff. If people make horrendous mistakes, we don't fire them. People get to leave only if they no longer have the support of the staff. We don't have to control them; nobody does. It turns out that if they don't have a good relationship with me (or with Carol), who is president of Actualizations then they won't have the support of the staff. But they are never subjected to the capricious whims and fancies of the boss in our organization.

If a particular person is not making the contribution he or she agreed to make, the other players notice. Then we get together and say, "Okay, the person who is playing this position is missing too many passes or isn't making enough yardage. What's that about?" And the whole staff explores what that is about. And if any member of the staff has a problem with that staff member, it is communicated. We do the workshop with the staff, so people can be clear on where they are and what would work for them.

Sometimes we find that what would support them is to not be there right now. If this happens, they get to be clear about the way in which the members of the staff experience them. Each member of the staff shares in a real and supportive way where he or she is with them. And it is presented in such a way that they can't ignore what is presented, they can't write it off as the capriciousness of one individual. And they are presented with the facts in a way in which they don't feel victimized.

We are always looking to keep the balance of contribution. It is an art, a dance.

Some people hold senior positions in the organization, not because they are better people or because they are smarter; they are simply willing to be accountable for a bigger part of the game. They are willing to be accountable, to stand up and be counted as a part. So the amount of the game the people are willing to stand up and be counted as a part of, agent of, or source of, determines how big a job they have—together, of course, with their ability to deliver what they said they would be accountable for.

Some Mistakes Businesses Make

One of the mistakes businesses often make is to let a person's strengths justify the weaknesses. Say for example that they have an outstanding salesman who drinks. They say, "It's all right that he drinks; he has great sales." Nonsense! People's strengths should not buy them absolution for their weaknesses. If they have great strengths, it makes their weaknesses even crazier. If they are so outstanding every other way, they should be inspired and supported in cleaning up their weaknesses.

The most unfair thing you can do to people is to give them jobs they have no real chance of accomplishing successfully. It absolutely destroys their self esteem. We have to set it up so that, as a result of their participation in the game, people have a broadening and deepening and growing experience of their own creative ability and know that they are doing something that truly makes a difference.

Don't Accept Problems Without Proposed Solutions

Too often, in managing people, we tend to come from a negative point of view. And when we do, everybody does.

When we play "Here Comes the Judge," everybody will play with us. When that happens, we tend to use problems to bring the game to a halt.

If the game is any good at all, there will be a surplus of problems. Unfortunately, we tend to view problems from a negative point of view. We see problems as trouble, rather than as opportunities. What it gets to look like is that all we do all day is pass problems back and forth. If we are employees, we besiege the boss with problems. We see the problem and then we go and dump it on the boss. If we are the boss, we besiege the employees with problems. The employees even consider *us* as one of their problems.

It is all a dramatization of "How do I avoid losing?" We figure, if there are enough problems, then it won't be our fault that it got screwed up. "After all, how could anything with that many problems ever succeed?" So, revealing all the problems is a way of proving that we didn't really lose. Nobody could have won with all those problems.

In our organization, we will not allow people to communicate problems unless, at the same time, they communicate a solution to the problem. The only exception we make to this rule is if it is an emergency and there is no time to come up with a solution. Barring emergencies, no one brings Carol or their manager a problem without having also brought along a solution.

This trains people to see problems as opportunities instead of as trouble, and to think for themselves, rather than rely on the boss as Santa Claus. They begin to see things in a positive, creative sense, rather than in a negative, "How do I avoid losing?" sense. And it doesn't have to be the right solution or the one we ultimately use. It just has to be *a* solution. This is important, because if people can't come up with a solution they feel good about, they may be tempted to hide the problem altogether. And buried problems have a way of exploding with painful repercussions.

A business organization should be founded on the principles of friendship. People can experience being part of a family; they can experience playing a game in which they are supported in being who they are and are not supported in being less than that. In this way, the organization becomes an opportunity for people to actualize their own qualities of personal excellence.

Together we can build a greenhouse in which we can all grow, in which we can discover each other's assets and use each other intelligently. We can manage each other in a way that allows our strengths to be put to the greatest and most productive use, and we are supported in letting those things go that don't really work for us.

What Happens When We Are the Employee

Why Would Anyone Hire Us?

The only reason people would hire us is because of the contribution they think we are going to make to the game and to their well-being. But we never think of that. What is on our minds when we go to a job interview is "What's in it for me?" Interestingly enough, nobody ever hired you for what's in it for you. You are hired because of what's in it for the other person. People hire us because of the contribution they perceive we are going to make to their well-being.

So if we really want to get hired, it would probably be smart to make sure that whoever is doing the hiring is clear about the contribution we see we can make. Doing that requires, of course, that we find out what contribution the person wants. So, in a hiring situation, we have to become clear about what's wanted and needed, and then let the prospective boss discover that we are the ones who can provide it.

It's Nothing Personal——Just Business

When the game is in progress, we must keep in mind that the boss is not so much interested in who is covering the positions as in making sure that all the positions are covered. So we need to recognize that when the game is in progress, people's positions are nothing personal. They are just positions that have to be played and have to be covered.

When we are the employee, we have got to recognize that it simply does not work to play the game from the position of "How do we prevent the boss from winning?" So often, that is where we are coming from: "Let's stop everybody from winning, particularly the boss. Let's make sure the boss doesn't make it." How often have you seen this in business?

We have to see that the boss is not our enemy. It's interesting; on the one hand we hope that the boss will be Santa Claus, and on the other, we treat him like the personification of the devil. Neither position works. Mostly we relate to the boss as if he were the enemy. We need to be willing to stop that. We need to be willing to support the boss in making it. If we are not willing for the boss to succeed, we will never succeed either.

It's All the Same

By now we should begin to see that the essence of all our relationships is exactly the same. There is no difference really in our relationships with ourselves, with our lover, with our parents, with our children, with our friends, or with our boss. It is all the art of being related. It is all the pursuit of the experience of unity. It is a very special, precious experience.

XII. HOW TO TRANSFORM
YOUR RELATIONSHIP
WITH REALITY

This Way to the Guru

A guru is a source of wisdom. More precisely, a guru is a source that supports another in coming into the experience of wisdom.

It has become very popular recently to be seeking after or sitting at the feet of some person whom we consider to be wise and who will lead us to the experience of our own wisdom. I think this is an important part of our evolution, and if that is what people are doing, I support them. As long as we don't turn a spiritual teacher into an enlightened form of Santa Claus.

I propose here that we use a different model for a moment. Let's say that the guru is not a who. Let's say the guru is a what. Let's say you are standing in the presence of the guru right now. The guru is physical reality.

Earlier, we looked at how what is going on around us is a reflection of our consciousness. We spoke about how we use life as a stage in which to cast, direct, and perform our own soap opera.

What I would like to look at now is how we can use the reality in which we function as a guru, as an indicator of how we are doing in life, as a way of seeing if the path we are on is workable or not. Let's find out how we can use reality to support ourselves in moving toward greater wisdom.

What Is Enlightenment?

I propose a definition of enlightenment. To me, we have reached a degree of enlightenment in an area of our lives when our relationship with life leads us in a direction of greater wisdom rather than in the direction of greater foolishness. That does not seem like such a big deal—except when you look more closely at it.

Reality supports our being wherever we are. If we say, "Fuck you," to life, life will. If we have an enormous outflow of negative energy, then there will be a lot of chaos, conflict, hostility, and unpleasantness in our surroundings. And if we flow in harmony with the natural order of the universe, where we are will be a little oasis that supports everyone who comes near it.

Since the planet supports our being wherever we are and since reality is a mirror, if we live in darkness the planet will support our being in darkness. We will have around us those things that we need to have in order to be in darkness. If we are traveling a path toward the light, the planet will support us in that.

So what becomes important is reaching the point where the planet is supporting our rise toward the light rather than our descent into darkness. When that happens, we are enlightened.

Is This Permanent Enlightenment?

Let's say you wanted to learn to play tennis. You could probably learn how to play without taking lessons, but that would be very slow. So let's say you take lessons.

Eventually as you practice and take lessons you will get to a point where you will no longer need to take lessons. You will have reached a stage in your enlightenment, regarding tennis, where just the participation in the game is in itself all the feedback you require to reach a higher level of art in the game of tennis. Your relationship with the game of tennis is all you need to become wiser and more enlightened at tennis. In a sense, you have arrived and you still have more to actualize. So, yes, there is a destination, and the destination is a spontaneous expansion that must be on going for the experience of "enlightenment" to stay with you.

Become a Master of Reality

In order to actualize our dreams, we have to become masters of reality.

That is a discovery that most people do not want to make. We occupy a physical body, we live in a physical universe, and our consciousness is reflected in physical forms.

Reality is a reflection of our consciousness. The measure of our consciousness is our ability to joyfully produce results in reality that are of service to ourselves, other people, and the planet we all share.

The forms in our lives are no more than a vehicle for our consciousness. They are not the source of our consciousness; they are a reflection of it. They are a statement of our consciousness. The forms that collect around us are a testimony to our consciousness. They are a metaphor for where we are.

Unless we find that out, we will never transform our relationship with reality. Reality will run us around in circles.

Everything You Wanted to Know About Failure but Were Afraid to Ask

Where to start: Fear of Failure

We seem to have a fear of interacting with reality, a fear of going forward and actually producing results in reality. It has been lumped loosely into one category called "fear of failure." But that doesn't tell us anything.

I received a marvelous education in this whole area of fear of failure on an airplane ride to Hawaii. The captain happened to be a friend of mine, and after we were airborne he invited me up to the flight deck to sit in his chair. Except for the landing, when I had to return to my own seat, I stayed in his chair for the entire flight.

Between the chair in which I was sitting and the chair where the co-pilot was sitting was a console that was supporting a tray of donuts and coffee. I thought this was its only purpose. The captain, whose name is Chuck, saw me looking at the console. "You want to see what's inside there?" he asked. I told him yes, and he opened it up. Inside was a little black box.

"It's the inertial navigation system," he said. "It tells us where we are. In the days of propeller-driven aircraft, we used to have human navigators. Then we started flying DC8's, which went at nearly the speed of sound, and that became a problem. By the time a human navigator would work out where we were, we weren't there any more. So we had to come up with a better system."

"This little black box tells us exactly where we are with almost zero time delay. And it simply tells us where we are. It does not say whether that's a good or a bad place to be; it's just where we are. It always knows where we're at. Not only that, but the little box always knows exactly where we are coming from, and it knows whether where we are is where we said we'd be in the flight plan. If there is a discrepancy, it lets us know exactly what to do to correct.

"This little black box," he continued, "literally uses the universe as a guru: it uses the universe as a source of wisdom about our position, because it plots our position relative to the other planets. It does not plot our position by looking into itself. It calculates where we are by looking outward at the world."

I said, "This is a marvelous analogy for people, because most of us try to figure out where we are by looking inside our heads."

"Yes," he said, "and therein lies the wisdom. This little black box will get us to within one thousand yards of the runway in Honolulu. It could get us within one thousand yards of a runway on the moon if we could fly to the moon. And that is only the beginning.

"I notice that you talk about people having this fear of failure. They have a fear of being foolish and are unwilling to be in error at all or to be caught in error, and they have a great sensitivity about being corrected.

"The fascinating fact is that we are going to get to Hawaii and we are going to touch down within five minutes of our estimated arrival time when we left. We will arrive in Hawaii on time, having been in error 90 per cent of the time along the way."

It is most important to realize that. A rocket to the moon spends 90 per cent of its time in error. If we could see that we can get a rocket to the moon and a 747 to Honolulu, having been in error 90 per cent of the time, we might be a little less uptight about being in error ourselves.

A sailboat cannot get from where it is to where it wants to be by traveling in a straight line. It has to zigzag. So, in terms of its true course, it is always in error. What is important about the sailboat, the rocket, and the 747 is that the errors cancel out.

So the path from here to where we want to be starts with an error, which we correct, which becomes the next error, which we correct, which becomes the next error, which we correct, and that becomes the next error, which we correct. So the only time we are truly on course is that moment in the zigzag when we actually cross the true path. The rest of the time, we are in error.

It was out of that story that I saw how sensitive we all are to being corrected, and how the way we respond to being corrected is a reflection of our own self-esteem.

I found myself imagining times that I'd been asked out to dinner. And I imagined that a lady had asked me out to dinner and was going to cook it at her place. Let's say she makes cannelloni.

I arrive at the appointed hour on the appointed day clutching red roses and a fine red wine, and we go through the pleasantries that people go through, and then we sit down and dinner is served.

The lady says to me, "Stewart, how's the cannelloni?" And I respond, "Well, it is great. I think that you make terrific cannelloni, and that probably you could have joined the ranks of the cannelloni maestros of the universe—if, the next time you make this dish, you added a half a glass of dry white wine and a tablespoon of fresh, chopped sweet basil to the sauce two minutes before you take it from the heat."

I speculated that what may very well happen is that I may find myself wearing cannelloni. There are two possibilities here. Possibility number one is that I don't know the first thing about cannelloni. In fact, I am so ignorant in culinary matters that I don't know the difference between cannelloni and a burrito. In which case, the lady has become upset from the input of a culinary fool. If she allows herself to become upset in response to the input of a fool, that places her in an area of even greater foolishness than the fool who gave her the input.

On the other extreme, the possibility is that I am one of the great culinary experts in the world. In which case, to be upset by input that was accurate, supportive, and in fact would transport her to among the ranks of the cannelloni maestros of this universe, would be inappropriate.

It is interesting that no matter what our response is to correction, any response that takes offense or is upset is inappropriate, no matter what position the person who offers the correction is coming from. If the person who gives you the correction is a fool, to be upset by a fool is to make yourself an even greater fool. If the input is of great value, to not consider it places you once again in the category of a fool.

So if you respond negatively to feedback, it is a reflection of your own foolishness and a reflection of your own absence of self-esteem in that area of your life.

My telling that to Chuck got him very excited. He said, "Well, I've got to introduce you to somebody else in the airplane." And the somebody else was the autopilot. Now, they call the inertial navigation system Fred, and the autopilot they call George. And we began to examine the relationship between Fred and George.

Their relationship is what in engineering terms is called a closed-loop feedback mechanism, which is just a fancy way of saying that Fred and George never get out of communication, that they always supply each other with feedback, they don't make each other wrong, and they don't take anything personally.

All the way to Hawaii, Fred and George have this conversation: Fred will say, "George, we're off course 2 degrees to starboard." And George will say, "Okay, Fred, I'll fix it."

"George, we're off course 3 degrees to port."

"Okay, Fred, I'll fix it."

"George, we're Dutch rolling."

"Okay, Fred, I'll fix it."

"George, we're forty knots below our airspeed."

"Okay, Fred, I'll fix it."

"George, we're three hundred feet below our corridor."

"Okay, Fred, I'll fix it."

And this conversation goes on all the way to Hawaii. Now, if Fred and George happened to be human beings in-

stead of technology, the conversation would probably go
something like this.

"George, we are off course 2 degrees to starboard."

"Okay, Fred, I'll fix it."

"George, we're off course 3 degrees to port."

"[Pause] . . . Okay, Fred, I'll fix it."

"George, we're Dutch rolling."

"All right, Fred, I will fix it."

"George, we're forty knots below our airspeed."

"Oh, for God's sake, Fred! Bitch, bitch, bitch! All you ever
do is bitch!"

The two people would take this all very personally. Yet
this feedback is the essence of the relationship that allows
that safe arrival of the airplane at Hawaii.

I could see that this was a very valuable lesson to learn.
And I began to look around for a way to translate this into
useful terms. And the inspiration came one evening a few
weeks later, when I was watching "Star Trek."

Yellow Alerts and Red Alerts

On "Star Trek" they have a marvelous system of red alerts
and yellow alerts. The yellow alert means things are about
to be not good and we better do something. If we don't do
something, then there is a red alert, which means things are
definitely going to get very bad very fast and if we don't get
it together we are going to be blown into interstellar space
by a Klingon battle cruiser. Of course, Captain Kirk and Mr.
Spock do get it together and it all turns out—until the next
rerun.

The Source of Failure

As I looked in my own life and at the lives of other people, I recognized that there are always yellow alerts and red alerts out there. They let us know how we're doing. If we look, we will see that there are little flags, little signposts, little alerts, say, "Hey, wait a minute, maybe you are off course" or "Wait a minute, maybe you ought to take a look and correct." And this told me something very basic about failure.

Failure, for the most part, is not a result of our lack of ability but a product of our basic lack of observation of the yellow and red alerts that pop up in life.

We are fundamentally no different from the 747 on its way to Hawaii or the rocket on its way to the moon. To be in life means that we are constantly off course. What is important is not that we are off course but whether or not we make the correction that needs to be made.

I see that most people don't make the necessary correction, because they are too busy being concerned with protection. Most people's failures in life are a product of protecting themselves when they should have been correcting themselves.

What they got out of the failure was the experience that they were not all right. It is not true that they weren't all right; they were just foolish because they did not look for and respond to the yellow alerts and the red alerts that the guru held up along the way—alerts that are almost like a flashing neon sign on the path of life.

It is almost as if people drive down the highway of life and suddenly notice that the gas gauge is near EMPTY. Instead of correcting—instead of pulling into a gas station—they cover up the gas gauge and pretend it isn't there—hoping that, when they wake up in the morning, God, Santa Claus, and the Easter Bunny will have filled the gas tank.

The unwillingness to be in error and correct is the source of most failures.

Successful people are like the 747 and the rocket. They are willing to live in error and they are willing to correct. They are people who are busily doing what they don't know for sure how to do. That's the adventure for them. They don't know what's around the next corner. All they know is that they are committed to the path and they will do whatever has to be done when they get around the next corner so they can get around the corner that's around the next corner.

Unsuccessful people just live intimidated and imprisoned by the fear of discovering that they are in error, or in the fear of finding out that they don't know for sure, or the fear of finding out that there is no certainty, no guarantee.

Spectrum of Failure

Anticipated Failure
Imminent Failure
Failure
Suppressed Failure
Causing Others to Fail

Failure can be divided into a spectrum just like the color spectrum of light. At the top of the spectrum of failure is something called *Anticipated Failure*.

Anticipated Failure is equivalent to a yellow alert. It simply means that we are in the place where we recognize that things are off course and that some correction should be implemented to bring them back on course. Successful people are willing to recognize that the correction is likely to take them off course in the other direction, like the swing of a pendulum, and they are willing to live with that. These people realize that Anticipated Failure and correction are their companions in life. They are always seeking to find the center of the swing of the pendulum—to find the balance.

Imminent Failure is next. Imminent Failure is a red alert. The best analogy I can think of is an automobile accident. If you have ever had one of that skidding kind of accident in which you reach a point where it becomes absolutely apparent to you that there's going to be a catastrophe but that it is going to take another one and a half seconds, you have experienced imminent failure. There is no way to avoid it. Now it is appropriate to protect, because it is too late to correct.

If you are flying an airplane and the thing is on fire, then you ought to bail out. That is an imminent failure. And when that happens, protection is the only course to take. But, remember, once we start protecting ourselves, we are in fact validating and guaranteeing the failure. When we are in Imminent Failure, the failure is not avoidable. We have a brief period of time in which we can minimize the loss, but the event called failure is not avoidable.

In fact, *Failure* is the next level on the spectrum. And that is simply the event. It is that event in which we did not get to where we said we were going to get to, or where we wanted to be. It just did not turn out. We failed.

Below Failure on the spectrum is *Suppressed Failure*. Here the failure has occurred but we suppress the experience of it in order to make it all right that we failed. "Well, I didn't really want to do that in the first place, anyway, and God knows best." "Everybody knows the economy was bad." "I like it better this way." It is all the things we do to pretend that it did not happen.

The lowest rung on the spectrum is *Causing Others to Fail*. Here we get to be all right by default. We cause all the people around us to fail so we end up being the least bad off. We are the least disastrous people we know, so we end up looking all right by comparison. We surround ourselves with losers so that among them we look like a winner.

Say Hello to Your Companion

What we discover is that to be in life is to have Anticipated Failure as a constant companion. Our path through life requires that we continuously survey the guru of the external universe, looking for the yellow alerts and the red alerts that tell us when we are in Anticipated Failure and had better correct or whether we are in Imminent Failure and had better protect.

We must learn to use the external physical universe to provide us with the feedback that enables us to navigate our way through life. *The only path from where you are to where you want to be is through the territory of Anticipated Failure.*

An Exercise

Take an event in your life that to you represents a significant failure. (If you haven't had one, go directly to Nirvana, do not pass GO.)

Describe the event to yourself. Then look for that moment in time at which the event that became a failure started as an idea. Then trace the time between the birth of the idea and the reality of the failure. Re-examine the path between the idea and the actual failure. You will start to notice all of the yellow alerts and red alerts that were there but that you ignored. Start to notice how you were more concerned with protecting yourself than you were with making corrections. You may also begin to notice all of the support you could have gotten that you wouldn't let yourself accept. You will start to see all of the feedback that was available to you, giving you an opportunity in ample time to discover that perhaps you were off course and letting you know what corrections would get you back on course.

We find out our path of failures is simply testimony to the way in which we did not respond to the signals that were clearly available had we been willing to see them, and we will see how many opportunities there were for correction had we been willing to take them.

It has been said that "All it takes for the forces of evil to win in the world is for enough good people to do nothing"—for enough good people to ignore the yellow alerts and red alerts and not actualize corrective action. There are a lot of yellow alerts and red alerts on the planet right now. But if history continues as it always has, we will ignore the obvious signals and continue in our foolishness. We will bury our heads and pretend that the problems before us on the planet will go away, and wait for Santa Claus and the Easter Bunny to take care of it, while we become preoccupied with protecting ourselves.

We have got to recognize that life is a constant experience of Anticipated Failure. We are born into a situation of Anticipated Failure. If we do not eat, we will not survive, we will fail to keep living—so eating itself is a correction of an Anticipated Failure.

If You Make Reality Your Enemy, You Lose

For the most part, we don't want to know about reality, really. We are hostile to anyone who suggests we look at it. We are hostile to anyone who holds up a flag that says, YELLOW ALERT, or RED ALERT. We simply don't want to know.

We want to live in our little dream world, where things are supposed to go better with Coke, where we are supposed to wake up in the morning to find that somebody has taken care of it all. And if it goes wrong, somebody will be there to tell us that it wasn't our fault.

We go blithely along pretending that it will all be okay, and yet deep down we have the gnawing anxiety that we are off course and that it probably will not turn out. But we continue as prisoners of hope.

A lot of people collectively have to make the discovery that we have nothing to gain and everything to lose if we make reality our enemy. Reality is really our friend, our companion who tirelessly and compassionately holds up signpost after signpost saying, "Hey, gang, you are off course." "Hey, Humanity, you really ought to correct." "Hey, folks, over here, listen to me, please." "Hey, my friends, I am not putting you down; I just really want you to hear me." Reality is our best friend and we continue to lumber forward in our ignorance, banging our heads on the universe. We never notice that it has so much to tell us. We are standing in the answer, wondering if there is an answer.

For some strange reason, we not only ignore or miss completely the signposts, we resent anyone who points them out to us. "He told me that what I am doing is not working, that troublemaker!"

If we look at some really successful event in our life, we will see the times that we were in Anticipated Failure, how many times we saw the yellow alerts and red alerts and responded.

The specter of failure, like fear, is not our enemy, it is our companion. Life is an experience of anticipating failure and correcting, anticipating failure and correcting. It is, as in surfing, a constant correction by using the movements of the waves as yellow alerts and red alerts.

If we are really going to get our life to turn out, we have to recognize that life is a joyful adventure and Anticipated Failure is our constant companion.

Recall for a moment the scale we spoke of earlier that went from *no fun* on the bottom to *actualization* on the top.

Actualization (that which is made real through action)
Clarity-power-enlightened action
wisdom-humor-simplicity

Viewpoint of accountability
Detachment from form
Commitment to your own well-being
Accept that a transformation is possible

Fear of worsening
Temporary well-being
Being a form junkie
No fun

Anticipated Failure is the middle ground between *no fun* and *actualization.* When we correct ourselves, we move up toward *actualization;* when we protect ourselves, we move down to *no fun.* The middle ground between the two extremes is a navigation process. Like walking a tightrope, our constant position is Anticipated Failure, and the tilt of the pole in our hands serves as the yellow alerts and red alerts to allow us to keep our balance, constantly correcting as we make our way to our destination.

Somehow people have the notion that they are going to get away from failure, that they are going to succeed enough to never fail again. That option is simply not available; it is like trying to eat once and for all.

People who are actualizing their essence are very skillful at seeing the yellow alerts and red alerts and implementing appropriate correction.

They recognize that life is not a riskless process. Most people simply do not want to know that. They don't want to know that when we got born all we got was a ticket to the game. We did not get a guarantee that we were going to like the game. The ticket just assures us that we are going to have an opportunity to like it or not like it.

Life is a fatal disease. The only thing certain about it is death. All the rest of life is uncertain. Most people prefer the certainty of a living death to the adventure of life's uncertainty.

Life is a joyful adventure. Each act is experimental, and the only way we can know how it works is to consult the guru—the external reality—for the yellow alerts and the red alerts, the signposts that really let us know how we're doing. Again, it's that great question from *Blazing Saddles* when we say, "Dear God, am I doing the right thing, or am I just jerking off?" Reality is always there to say, "Hey, guess what. . . ." And we get a chance to correct. If we don't, we crash and burn.

Life is simple, though not always easy.

XIII. TRANSFORMING YOUR RELATIONSHIP WITH LIFE

The Pursult of Purposes and Goals

Earlier in the book, we made the distinction between living and life. We said that living is about surviving, it is about the mechanics of existence. Living includes such things as eating, sheltering oneself, clothing oneself, paying the phone company, and other things like that. Living is about maintaining the conditions that allow life to exist. The only purpose for getting living handled is to experience life.

Life, as we said, is a journey in which we go from occupying a minute part of reality to being able to embrace all of reality. Life is about the experience of the reality of the fundamental nature of the universe.

Why Have Goals Become a Rip-off?

Goals have become a rip-off to us because we see them as a solution to life, when they can never be more than a solution to living.

We have the implicit belief in goals the same way we have the implicit belief in Santa Claus. It is the continuing saga of our addiction to form. We still firmly believe that something outside of ourselves is going to make us happy.

"If I get a million dollars, I'll be happy."

"If I get a new car, then I'll be happy."

"If I get a new job, then I'll be happy."

"If I get straight A's in school, then I'll be happy."

"If I get my Ph.D., then I'll be happy."

"If only ———, then I'll be happy." You fill in the blank.

Goals have become part of that whole happiness-through-acquisition belief program that everybody has bought. It works this way: For most of us, life floats between terrible and bearable, but there is hope—hope that life will be more bearable if we achieve a goal exterior to ourselves. As if the destination itself will have any effect upon the traveler.

The fact is that goals do not deliver what we are asking and expecting them to deliver. That has become a source of disillusionment and dissatisfaction in our society. Every time we reach a goal, we have a momentary feeling of ela-tion (temporary well-being) followed by a sinking realiza-tion that nothing fundamental has really changed. Here we are with what we said we wanted, but without the experi-ence that getting what we said we wanted was going to bring us. Ripped off again.

All a goal does is alter the circumstances in which you are the way you are. It does not fundamentally alter the way you are. It is true that we may alter on the way to the goal, but that is a function of our movement, not a function of achieving the goal.

Now we have revealed something about goals. On the one hand, we need to have them, they are a part of living. And on the other hand, they are a continual source of disap-pointment and disillusionment. So we have built up a nega-tive case against the pursuit of goals. We say they are a part of the "consumerist society." "People who pursue goals are too materialistic. The preoccupation with the pursuit of goals is why life does not work."

That of course is ridiculous. Life doesn't work, because we don't know what life is about. Our style of living—the way we go about not having life work—doesn't make much difference.

What Is a Goal, Anyway?

A goal is nothing more than the excuse for the game. That is all a goal is—the excuse for the game.

In football, the excuse for the game is to get this funny, egg-shaped ball between what we have to agree are the two most significant posts on the planet. In fact, the posts and the area between them are called the *goal*. Now, if you stop and think about it, football is a silly game.

Obviously, your experience of life will not be better if you get the ball between the two posts. If getting the ball between two posts would make life better, then everybody could go and get a ball and put it between two posts. You could say, "Okay, fellas, I am going to transform my life, go down to the store and buy me a ball, then go out and find two posts and put the ball between them: then I'll wait for it all to happen."

It sounds crazy, but that is what is going on. A lot of people out there are looking for something magic to happen when they put a ball between two posts. And, of course, nothing happens.

So, if we re-examine the game, we say, "Wait a minute;

what the game is about is the process; what it's about is what you have to go through to get the ball between the two posts."

If you don't have any fun getting the ball between the two posts, then actually getting the ball there will not make any difference. If you had a bad time getting the ball between the two posts, when you do get the ball between the two posts, the only elation you will feel is the kind of elation you experience when you stop hitting your head against a brick wall. It certainly feels better when you stop, but it doesn't alter or transform the fundamental quality of your existence.

All you will have when you get the ball between the two posts is a ball between two posts. It is the fact that people don't get that, which allows goals to be the rip-off they have become.

On a material level, it is harder to see. For people who don't have an automobile, telling them that they won't be better off if they get an automobile is ridiculous. Because they *will* be better off in terms of living. But, in terms of life, it will make no difference at all.

It would be easier for someone to understand who was upgrading from a Chevrolet to a Buick or from a Buick to a Cadillac. That person could possibly understand that it is not going to make any difference. If people are living in scarcity and are materially impoverished, you cannot expect them to hear this. And I don't think it serves them to tell them, because at a very practical level, their life *would* be more comfortable, or easier, or more convenient.

If they reach a certain level of acquisition, then they will begin to hear you, because they will get enough stuff to know that getting more stuff will not make a difference.

Goals really are no more than an excuse for the game. I

really mean that. They are an excuse to participate and relate at a very, very deep level. The game is simply a form we adopt which occupies time and space while our essences, our spirits, interact. The only part of us that can really have a relationship is our spirit, our being, or our essence.

The Myth of Independence

We have the mistaken idea that, by achieving a goal, we will become independent, we can get to the place where we won't need anybody any more. It is the American myth of the rugged individualist. Being independent and not needing anybody is very American. Here is the biggest mistake of them all, because the truth is you can't make it by yourself.

It is very un-American to say that you cannot make it by yourself. But to the extent that people pursue a course of action designed to demonstrate they can make it by themselves, the attainment of each goal along that path is a step into further darkness.

If we are to transform this planet, then enlightenment will have to be considered as people's birthright, rather than the experience of a fortunate few. But, you see, for most of us, living is not about enlightenment; it is about endarkenment. Most people are busily pursuing a path of endarkenment, and a lot of the path of endarkenment is paved with goals about which people have expectations that cannot possibly be met, particularly the goal of independence, because every goal along the path to independence lends credence to the fact that it is possible to be independent. And we don't get independent; we get more separated. That is absolutely the path of endarkenment.

Being independent is being separate. And the more independent we become, the further we move away from the unity we need to experience if we are going to make it as a species. It is an incredible trap. There are some very successful people in the "Let's Reach the Goal" game who live in absolute darkness.

By the way, there is another trap. As long as we think that Things go better with goals, then if we don't get them, things will go worse.

What Do You Want Out of Life?

When you ask that question of people they often say, "I want to be happy."

That is an unsatisfactory goal.

If you make the purpose and goal of your life to be happy, happiness will elude you. Happiness, or having fun, cannot be the aim in life.

If you walk into hotel casinos such as the ones in Las Vegas, you will see many of the people there trying to have fun. If you look at their faces, you will see that what they call fun is simply indulging in diversionary tactics that take them away from the experience of pain. The best life gets for them is when they don't notice that it hurts. They do whatever they need to do to prevent themselves from noticing how much it hurts. Ask them how they are doing and they are likely to say something like, "Feeling no pain." That is what we get when we make the purpose of life to be happy or to have a good time.

What Is the Purpose of Life?

We could really get into some trouble if we presumed to tell people what the purpose of their life is. I have a sense of what the purpose of my life is, and here it is: To respond in a workable fashion to whatever happens to be in front of me at the moment—recognizing that I may not have much choice about what is in front of me.

We discussed earlier in the book that what's in front of us are the lessons we each have to learn. If we take the Eastern philosophical view, then we may have come into life with our karmic lessons to learn. If we take the purely Western view, then the lessons before us are the product of our conditioning.

We can't even really make comparisons between my lessons and yours. Your lessons are not senior to mine, and mine are not senior to yours. Wherever people are in their evolution, their lessons are of the same magnitude to them as yours are to you. One person may be operating at a much higher level than another person, but relative to where they are, their individual lessons have the same degree of significance.

It is easy to judge someone else's process and say, "Well, that's nothing. I can't understand why that person is struggling with that. I gave up struggling with that bullshit ten years ago." That is a terrible putdown; what he or she is confronting is as big a struggle for that person as our current struggle is for us.

The truth of the matter is that you've got in front of you what you've got in front of you, and I've got in front of me what I've got in front of me, and knowing how or why is totally irrelevant. The lessons are there. Let's get on with it.

All we have is a choice about whether we are going to respond or not. Are we going to learn the lesson or are we going to ignore the lesson? Are we going to regard it as an adventure or are we going to regard it as a struggle?

That is the central question. How are we going to respond to what is in front of us?

Now, it may turn out that for us, life is about finding out what our program is and getting with it. Many people never get with their program, because they never find out what their program is.

We have had our mother and our father telling us what the program is supposed to be, we have had our kindergarten teacher telling us what it is supposed to be, we have had our college professor telling us, and for many of us, we have had our psychiatrist telling us what our program is supposed to be. So there we are. We have in front of us the lessons we have to learn. Are we going to learn them or not? My sense of things is that our happiness is tied up in whether or not we learn the lessons before it's too late.

There is no question in my mind that Shakespeare was an enlightened man writing about the process of enlightenment. And in all the plays of Shakespeare it is easy to see the lessons before each of the principal players. If they get enlightened before the social process of their existence reaches the point of no return, the play is a comedy. If they reach enlightenment after they arrive at the point of no return, then it is a tragedy.

In terms of the things we have been talking about in this book, it is a difference between getting enlightened in Anticipated Failure or getting enlightened in Imminent Failure. If you get enlightened in Imminent Failure, all you can do is enjoy the crash, and recognize that it's all going to be over in the next little while, and so you might as well surrender to the end of your life this time, and hope that next time you have the sense to learn the lessons in time.

If we get enlightened in Anticipated Failure, then life becomes a response to what's in front of us. If we can make responding to what is in front of us a game, just as we make tennis and golf a game, then life takes on a completely different kind of glow. Our joy and our satisfaction and our happiness are a product of the way in which we play the game, for which a goal is purely an excuse.

If we are going to come up with a goal or a purpose that works, it would have to be something along the lines of "training ourselves to respond to the lessons we have in front of us as an adventure, as an opportunity of discovery rather than as a threat." And then let's get on with the game. Only then will it start to turn out.

Then the purpose becomes the compassionate understanding and acceptance of our own process—the acceptance of the lessons in front of us. We must learn to accept the path before us and look at it with wisdom, humor, and simplicity. Once we accept our own process, we can begin to be aware of the processes that other people are confronting.

Ordinarily, we never take the time to notice other people's processes. We are so embroiled in trying to figure our way out of the complexity of our own process that we never take the time to notice what other people are struggling with in their own lives. But that is where freedom lies. It lies in surrendering to the lessons of our own process and in contributing the wisdom gained along our own path to other people for use in learning the lessons that are in front of them, and to gratefully and gracefully accept the wisdom of those who have passed this way before us. We must recognize that we each have our own path, but we can walk them together.

For the most part, we are too busy resenting our lessons, resisting them, making them wrong, trying to change them, or trying to figure out where they came from; we are too busy thinking about our process to actually get on with it and rejoice in our path.

If we play the game as a game, if we can see it as an adventure, if we are willing to experiment, if we are willing to take risks, "to boldly go where no man has gone before" as they put it in "Star Trek," and if we remember to laugh at how serious we can make it, then we are alive.

I am certain we will not discover life on other planets until we discover life on this one.

Most people operate in life as if they were alone. One of the great things about the workshop is that we find out that we are not alone, that all have their process. They have their lessons to learn, and they all have their own stuff going on with them. So we can stop putting ourselves down for having our process. We begin to accept it and stop believing that we will be through with it someday. We begin to discover that really all that is available to us is an alteration in our response to our process, not an alteration in the process itself.

We have talked about life and our life goals in very general terms. Now we need to get more specific.

What Do We Really Want?

The way we can best discover what we really want is to write what we *think* we want down on paper, or on 3-by-5 cards, or on a blackboard. It needs to be visible. We need to hang out with what we think we want and find the origin of that want. The aim is to find out whether we are the source of the want or whether it is something that we were told we wanted.

In other words, we have to begin by owning our own wants, which is something we have probably never done. We have to discover which wants are there because we thought that was what we were supposed to want.

As we start to become aware of the difference between our own wants and those that we collected from outside of us, we become able to own our experience and the way in which our wants relate to our experience. We will start perhaps to discard a lot of wants (actually, they are more accurately called "acquisition goals," because we never really wanted them in the first place. We only wanted them because we were told we did or we thought we ought to. We have been conditioned to want them).

So, suddenly, we may find that many of the things we thought we wanted, we don't—which may make us feel a lot better. In the process of looking at all the things you have said you want, you may end up saying, "Well, wait a minute. I don't think I really want that, anyway. I have been trying to get all the things my parents wanted that they never got which they told me I wanted so they could get at them vicariously through me. . . ."

If we start to examine our wants experientially, we become very clear that really what we want is the thing we have talked about many times during this book: we want an experience of ourselves as a lovable and capable person. Notice we are not saying a happy person; we're not necessarily saying a satisfied person or a fulfilled person. Certainly happiness, satisfaction, and fulfillment are very good yardsticks and very good indicators that we feel lovable and capable.

But sometimes, while we are feeling lovable and capable, it is very painful, because we're in the midst of a difficult lesson for us.

If we examine our wants, we will soon start to see how our needs and wants relate to us in terms of our experience of ourselves as lovable and capable people, and we will start to differentiate those wants the pursuit of which really represents movement along our process and those wants the pursuit of which represents our attachment to comfort and to the avoidance of fear.

We will start to become sensitive to the needs and wants that if pursued lead on to enlightenment, and the needs and wants that if pursued lead on to endarkenment. Not that any specific want is necessarily an enlightening one or an endarkening one, except in the way it relates to our particular process. What would be a goal or want for you that would lead you to the next step up the ladder of enlightenment, may for me represent the next step down the ladder of endarkenment, because each lesson is no more than a step.

We will start to recognize the kinds of activities that work for us—the kinds of relationships, the kind of pastimes, the kinds of games within the game that really generate an experience of more and more light and more and more awareness.

We can actually discover what it is we like to do, and what activities lead on to an enlightening experience of our existence and what activities lead on to an endarkening experience of our existence.

And all it takes is the willingness to write down our wants, examine each goal, each need, each want, see what its origins are and what expectation we have regarding what our experience will be if we should happen to achieve it.

I think the perfect example of that is the story, of the man who wanted to become a woman, that we discussed earlier in the book. He thought that what he wanted was to become a woman, and what we did in the workshop was to trace the origins of that want. He got to the point where he recognized that the satisfaction of that want would in no way satisfy the origins of the want. He learned to distinguish between the form of the want and the essence of it. He thought that what he wanted was to become a woman. What he really wanted was to get rid of the pain he carried inside. But he had long since forgotten that that was his original motivation. What he was now preoccupied with was the form called becoming a woman. And as soon as he could get that the source of the pain was his mother's craziness, and that it was nothing personal, he could see that becoming a woman would solve nothing for him.

So, to repeat, we write down all our wants, needs, and goals—all the things we want in terms of material acquisitions and in terms of things we want to do and want to be. Then we search within ourselves to determine the origin.

We need to ask ourselves such questions as, "If I do this or get this, what contribution do I think it is going to make to my life? Is that realistic or not?"

We need to remember that goals do not work until we see them as merely an excuse for the game. As long as we are looking toward the goal as something that's going to make it intrinsically better when we get to it, it will be a rip-off.

Getting On with It

The other thing we need to do is to get more immediacy into our lives. Normally we operate under the illusion that life lasts forever. The things that are really important to us get lost. Our real goals and purposes get buried under our preoccupation with the form of living. So we never get to the essence of our goals and purposes.

Elisabeth Kubler-Ross has done enormously valuable research into the nature of dying. And she has made the discovery that the people who have the greatest difficulty with dying are those who have never lived. The members of the living dead have great difficulty about the specter of their own departure. While those who have lived in life and have enjoyed it with a passion are kind of all right about it all: "Well, it's something that is going to happen, and it's okay."

Those people who have really lived don't feel as though they are going to miss anything or that they are being cheated. Those who have never really lived, on the other hand, when confronted with the notion of their own death are flooded with all the experiences they never acknowledged, never shared, never participated in, never really experienced. They remember all the people they never said, "I love you," to, all the people they never let themselves open up to, all the times they wanted to and didn't. They become aware of how much of the time they have been living separated from the experience of their own essence and from the experience of the essence of others. Suddenly, when it is too late, life suddenly takes on an enormous meaning and is seen as a magical opportunity but an opportunity that has passed them by before they were willing to see what it was. I see that on a lot of people's faces—the preoccupation with the worry of about how sad we will be when we come to the end and realize we could have done much more with what we were given. To find out too late that life can be a song to be sung, rather than a sentence to be served.

This is all a result of being in Anticipated Failure and protecting instead of correcting. When we discover that we could be getting on with it and we haven't, we have a choice: We can now get it on, or we can continue to punish and flagellate ourselves for not having gotten it on before this. We can walk away from the prison and into life, or we can stay and throw stones at our former cage. The door is open. The choice is ours.

What If I Had Just Six Months to Live?

Really! Think about that one. What would you do if you really knew that you had just six more months to be in this life? Sit down and look at your life from that perspective. You may re-evaluate your own life goals. Some people who have terminal illnesses really go and do all the things they have always wanted to, and the terminal illness miraculously disappears.

It seems clear that much of our illness is a function of having suppressed our own essence. Finally, after years of spiritual death, our body goes into agreement with us. The body can no longer support being owned by a spiritually dead person. The body finally says, "Okay, I have to agree with that and die also."

The purpose of looking at ourselves as if we had only six months to live is really to get a sense of urgency and immediacy back into our lives. If you really had just six months to live, you might stop everything and go and do what you've always wanted to do. It might be more appropriate to look at what you would do if you had only six months, then figure out a way to do those things within the next three years.

The purpose of this exercise is to bring up all those things that we really want to do but are putting off because we have the mistaken notion that life goes on forever.

I think that *Zorba the Greek* is a book that everyone would get enormous value out of reading. It traces the relationship between Zorba, who was fully alive, and the Englishman, who was trapped in the traditions of how one should live. That is the way it is with all of us. We are taught to despise our own experience. We get so much information about the way we should be that is in direct conflict with our inner experience, with what our essence is so loudly trying to tell us, that some of us actually die to resolve the conflict.

We are taught early in life to deny our own experience and to embrace outside opinions. We have an inner experience of what works, but it is often in conflict with what our mother or teachers have told us. Rather than threaten the form of our relationship with our mother by communicating our experience, we invalidate our experience: we swallow the truth inside of us and withdraw further into our own heads and away from life. If we would say something like, "Look, I don't want to live the way you think one should live. If you insist on living that way, then you and I can't live together," she is going to be hurt because she is certainly going to take that personally. We will have destroyed everything upon which she has constructed her existence. So many times, we have had to make the choice as children between our love for our parents and the sanctity of our own, inner experience.

It is this kind of conflict in life that makes us desire so strongly to be "independent." That looks a lot like a solution to the problem of conflict. But we cannot experience ourselves independently. The fundamental nature of the universe is relationship. The fundamental law of the universe is that everything is in relationship to everything and there is a harmonious balance.

The pain and conflict drives us toward being independent. We make independence a lofty goal. And if we achieve a degree of what we call independence, we find we are separate from the pain and the conflict but we are also separate from the joy and the satisfaction and the love and the happiness.

If we are going to make it, we need to look at the goal conflicts in our life and resolve them. We need to recognize the difference between goals that contribute to life, and those that merely add to our entanglement in the form of living. I am not against forms. There are forms that support our experience and our process in life, and there are those forms which entangle us and make us less able, less competent, less spontaneous in life. We just need to learn the difference.

So part of what life is about is discovering that we cannot make it alone. At some level, we really do need each other. More than that, we really *are* each other. I am not talking about need in terms of dependency or in terms of Santa Claus, but in terms of accountability. I simply cannot have all of myself in isolation; I need people and the world as a mirror to see myself.

Each person and the kaleidoscopic forms of the world reflect to me an aspect of myself. But people and the world cannot function for me as a mirror as long as they exist for me as a threat. To grow taller than the threat, we must grow beyond dependence and preoccupation with the avoidance of loss. We will then arrive at independence. Which is a trap unless we see it as a prelude to the master game: the art of creative interdependence, the art of playing together in reality, creating results of joyful service, and being mirrors to each other's enlightenment.